Magical Healing
TREES
in SLAVIC FOLKLORE

RONESA AVEELA

BENDIDEIA
PUBLISHING

Contents

Deep-rooted Beliefs

To send something to Tililei Forest (Тилилейска Гора) is to send it to a place where all bad things go.

Since ancient times, civilizations have considered trees and nature sacred. Whenever I drive through the countryside in the New England area in autumn, I can appreciate why trees have inspired awe. The hillsides are awash with a multitude of colors, God's patchwork quilt placed lovingly upon the land. Simply walking in the midst of a forest gives me a sense of peace and security.

A Bulgarian saying goes, "There is a sacred forest but no sacred field." Fields were where the people toiled so they could survive. It was a part of their everyday lives. But the forest was the mystical, the unknown. It held dangers. To venture there purposefully when not in search of food was to seek a spiritual awakening.

According to sources from the tenth century, the Slavs practiced what was called the cult of the trees. People prayed to the plants towering above them. Beneath the shade of these age-old trees were places where villagers held rituals that honored both life and death, and it was believed that the tree died and came back to life every year. In some cases, it was recorded that worshipers let the blood of sacrificial animals soak into the roots. Although other accounts state that the areas in which these sacred trees were found were safe zones where no blood could be shed—not even during war. The people also made confessions at the roots of the trees. In return, the trees listened, even though they could not reply.

It wasn't so much the trees themselves that were worshipped, but the deities or spirits housed within them. They were considered village patrons, protecting the people from adversities, such as hail, fire, and other natural disasters. Among some of the Slavs, people desired to have the tree spirit protect their home. If it was a new house being built, the spirit would enter through the wood planks cut from the tree. Homeowners had to be cautious, however, and use only those trees in which good spirits dwelled and avoid the ones demons inhabited. Trees also held certain qualities, such as prosperity, knowledge, health, happiness, and life. Therefore, when the wood was used for household items, it retained these qualities.

Another attribute of trees was the distinction between dry and green wood. Green was good and meant health and prosperity. On St. George's Day, it was customary to hang swings on trees and swing for health, prosperity, and success. However, the trees and branches had to be green and healthy. If someone swung on a dry tree, they believed the person would die within the year.

Dry trees and leaves were associated with witches. These malicious people would stick dry leaves into the wall of homes or into the corners of buildings and chant, "As these leaves have dried up, so let the owner and his children dry up with the whole house." Dry becoming green, however, was a sign of forgiveness, redemption, and rebirth.

Age-old trees have been treated with respect throughout the ages. Sacred groves within forests were often places that were fenced off and held a shrine of some sort in the center. In addition to the tree, such places could contain a Christian chapel or cross.

It was forbidden to cut down these sacred trees, break or cut their branches, cause them any damage, or even remove the fallen trees or their deadwood from the area. Those people who disobeyed suffered calamities: crop failure, livestock pestilence, and even the person's death. People believed that a tree, like humans, should die on its own. Cutting the tree was like committing murder.

A nineteenth-century account tells how one man ordered an ancient oak to be chopped down. The falling tree crushed him to death. Not only that, but afterward, a thunderstorm raged for a week, causing extensive damage to the village. I talk about my own experience with my father cutting down an ancient tree a little more in the next chapter.

As Christianity made its way into the lands where Slavs lived, certain records indicate that people begged the priests not to chop down the trees. One account tells how the people allowed images of their gods to be destroyed, stating that the gods could defend themselves if they had any divine power. If they couldn't even defend themselves, how would they be able to defend the people? But when it came time to destroy the tree that was held sacred to that divinity, the people objected. The tree itself, they said, was not sinful, and it provided not only shade, but livelihood and sustenance. The people promised that their desire was to save the tree, rather than being saved by the tree. If the Christian priest allowed the tree to stand, the villagers would no longer attach any divinity to the tree, nor would they offer sacrifices there.

World Tree

Trees rise high above the land, spreading their branches to the sky and digging their roots deep into the ground. Some species, like oak, ash, linden, willow, maple, sycamore, and walnut, are bestowed with the title of "World Tree," an honor making them like a supreme god among trees. This deeply venerated tree was seen as a force of strength and protection.

The World Tree or Tree of Life symbol is often depicted in Slavic art, such as embroidery, weaving, and stone and wood carvings. As far back as ancient Assyria, a palmetto or date palm represented the Tree of Life to demonstrate the power of life. Often, springs or fountains were included in the symbols. It made its way to the Balkans from

Byzantium, and obtained the Christian symbolism of eternal life, resurrection, and the eternal soul.

Among the Slavs, the World Tree was mainly a giant oak. The three parts of the tree symbolize the nature of the universe. The crown represents the heavens and all its inhabitants: birds, as well as divine spirits. Perun, the supreme god, sat at the top, depicted as an eagle. The trunk signifies Earth, the home of men, animals, and preternatural creatures like nymphs and fairies. And roots represent the underworld, the realm of the dead, and creatures like snakes, fish, and dragons, which may embody demons or other beings of darkness. It was here, among the roots, Volos, god of the underworld, was found, often shown as a snake.

Another interpretation of the three parts of the World Tree relates to humankind. The roots are ancestors, the trunk is those currently alive, and the leaves and branches are the future generations. As the leaves continue to be renewable, so will the people continue to exist.

Since the World Tree sat at the boundary of all three realms, it was viewed as the means to traverse from one to the other. This concept is often portrayed in fairy tales. It is through one of these World Trees that people access the otherworld, the land of the dead. If a demon stole a woman's child and replaced it with the demon's own child, the woman would bring the child to the age-old tree and leave it there, returning later to collect her own child from the same location. Other than people, objects could also be sent to the otherworld by throwing them at the tree. In particular, these would be things that had a connection with the deceased.

Perhaps the best-known World Tree to the western world is the Norse Yggdrasil. As far as I know, the Slavs do not give their World Trees a particular name, but different trees

species are called World Trees, a primary one being the oak. In our middle-grade fantasy series, we call the World Tree in Dragon Village (Zmeykovo) the Znahar Tree, since *znahar* is the word for a wise old woman who heals with herbs and charms. The Firebird roosts in this tree, protecting it. The eagle is another animal you may find within the branches of Slavic World Trees. Both birds are considered messengers of the gods.

Prevalent[1] in many creation myths is a cosmic tree, or a World Tree, that grows out of the water and supports the land. It's known by various names: "tree of life, tree of knowledge, tree of the Garden of Eden, tree of the cross, Shaman's tree" (Georgieva, 30). It's also been called "a golden fruit bearing tree," a "straight tree—tall and lean," and a tree whose branches are "pure silver, dotted with golden bees" (Zhelev).

Many illustrations display the serpent coiled at the tree's roots or along its trunk. However, in popular belief, it can also live in the tree's crown as a dragon—thus showing the creature's dichotomy of being both an evil viper and a benevolent guardian. Also inhabiting the branches are magical birds, such as the firebird (the messenger of divine will and the protector of the fruit of life, the magic apple), nightingale, falcon, and eagle (the symbol of light and heaven). Other birds found there include doves, swallows, roosters, and peacocks. Even bees make their home in the tree's branches.

The snake and the bird are the most widespread personifications of a human soul. This belief relates to the shaping of the idea about two worlds of death—one below the earth and another above the clouds. Therefore, the images of snake and bird merge to create the winged dragon (Georgieva, 68).

Over time, the benevolent dragon and the eagle have become interchangeable in folklore, thus associating the dragon with both heaven and earth as a cosmic mediator between the two. And so, from serpent to dragon, the creature becomes connected to all three parts of the universe: the roots and the dead, the trunk and the living, the branches and the divine beings.

- **The Dead**. The World Tree has been called the "Path to the Souls of the Ancestors" (Israfela), and it symbolizes "the transformation and transition between the worlds" (Israfela). It's a place where the souls of the dead reside, and a place from which one can enter the realm of the ancestors, often called the "other world" or the "beyond." This is a place where not only the dead, but also mythical creatures, live.
- **The Living**. The World Tree has a place in the daily lives of people. It underlines "the inseparable connection between the cosmic balance, life—fertility—marriage—death" (Israfela). Many life-cycle rituals involve trees—especially fruit-bearing trees, symbolic of this World Tree.

---

[1] The following is an excerpt about the Slavic World Tree from our book, *A Study of Dragons of Eastern Europe.* Original sources used are cited at the end of the chapter.

- **The Divine**. Among the Slavs, the World Tree is often oak and sacred to the god Perun, wielder of thunder (who in later beliefs becomes St. Iliya or Elijah, who fights against destructive dragons). In folklore, the tree may also be a cypress or sycamore.

Sacred Forests

One of the most magical places in Bulgaria is the sacred site of Krustova Gora, Holy Trinity Cross Forest, located in the Rhodope Mountains in the southern part of the country. This site holds great spiritual significance and is well known for its healing power. The place gives you a sense you're touching the mystery of nature. What gives it this ability is a piece of Christ's cross, which stories say lies buried there at a location where the mountain forms the shape of a cross.

It's interesting to note that the symbolism of the cross predates Christianity. In many ancient cultures, the cross has been viewed as portraying the tree of life, as well as being associated with the sun and fire. Among the ancient Thracians, the four directions of the cross have specific meanings. Although left has often been considered "sinister" in some cultures (and, in fact, the word sinister comes from the Latin word meaning "left"), among the Thracians, that direction was the more sacred of the two.

Right and left to them represented the earthly and celestial realms, respectively. Rituals in which actions took place from right to left were ones that took the participant from a lower level of consciousness to a higher one. This was standard practice in blood sacrifice rituals and enabled a sick person to become filled with power.

North and south were also sacred directions among the Thracians. North was the direction associated with mankind and south for immortals and the souls of the blessed. Rituals that included right-to-left and north-to-south movements were an attempt to unify the earthly and heavenly realms with the goal of providing healing.

The holy relic at Krustova Gora is said to be the one that Saint Helena gave to her son, Emperor Constantine. According to one story, this piece of the cross made its way to Krustova Gora after a Russian tsar seized it from a Turkish sultan. Believing that the relic brought his troops and empire victories, the sultan sent his troops after the Russians. The latter had changed their route and arrived at Krustova Gora and left the relic with the monastery. The monks living there buried the piece of the cross before they were killed during the subsequent invasion.

Church tradition states that Helena had gone in search of Christ's tomb and discovered it in 326. She placed the cross in the church of the Holy Sepulchre in Jerusalem, but kept a piece. On September 13, 335, the church was consecrated. The next day, the cross was displayed outside the church, where a congregation of people could venerate it.

In honor of this event, on the eve of September 14, Holy Cross Day or Feast of the Cross (official name of Universal Exaltation of the Precious and Life-Creating Cross), many

pilgrims travel to Holy Trinity Cross Forest. The site is said to be filled with unexplained, extraordinary power that can cure any sickness.

The magical powers are at their peak on the evening of September 13, the night before the Day of the Cross. People believe the heavens will open, and Jesus will descend to Earth to grant the wishes and cure the illnesses of those who offer prayers with true faith. Many stories tell how people with cancer and other incurable diseases miraculously found a cure. They say the water in the vicinity cures skin diseases and helps women conceive.

Those seeking God's blessings climb the mountain peak for a vigil that ends when the sun touches a metal cross that has been erected there. This time of year is associated with the arrival of autumn, when the sun begins its journey toward winter. In mythology, it is the day when day and night crisscross, being of equal duration, called the crossover of the sun.

People also believe the extraordinary healing energy of Cross Forest comes from an ancient sanctuary to Dionysus, which is said to be hidden somewhere in the forest. But the Rhodope Mountains keep their secrets.

Spiritual Abode

In folklore, many magical creatures such as fairies dwelled within the forest. Some of them had specific trees which they inhabited. Rusalki, female water spirits, could be found among birches and willows, while Samodivi, forest nymphs, were more likely to frolic around trees with large, sprawling branches. Demons lurk within thorny branches, and the Devil himself hides in the hollow of elderberry branches or willows.

These magical creatures knew the secrets of nature. Some would willingly teach their wisdom to humans whom the fairies deemed worthy. Other times, knowledge was tricked or forced from the magical beings.

Fairies were not the only ones who lived within trees, however. The ancient gods were believed to dwell there as well. Often, the god to whom the tree was dedicated resided there only in spirit. At times, a literal image of the god was placed within the trunk of a tree. *The Life of Saint Otto* describes an account about a time when pagan priests smuggled away a golden image of the three-headed Slavic god Triglav. They brought the idol to a widow who kept it safe at her farm, where the priests did not think anyone would come in search of it. The widow made a hole in the trunk of a large tree, wrapped the statue in a blanket, and placed Triglav inside the enclosure, so that no one could see or touch the idol. A small hole remained in the trunk where worshipers could insert their offerings. The widow placed the statue so firmly inside that a person sent to retrieve the idol through deceit could not reclaim or even move it.

Souls of the dead were also believed to live within trees. At one time, Slavic burial customs involved wrapping the deceased in birch bark and later on in hollowed-out oak logs. But that did not necessarily mean those souls were transferred into the trees. This belief more likely stems from the fact that those who died an unnatural death were buried under forest trees, away from sacred ground. In some places, those who committed suicide could not have a cross placed over the grave; instead, a tree could be planted. Fruit trees, however, were more likely to be planted on those who died normal deaths. It was believed that the person's soul passed into the tree.

In folk songs, the souls of the deceased seek blessings from the Tree of Life. They beg it to stretch down its branches to them. This will enable the souls to step onto the branches so they can cross over a sea that separates the world of the living from that of the dead.

From the tree itself, one could sometimes tell what kind of soul it possessed. Birch trees were reserved for the souls of girls. If the birch grew intertwined with another tree, this signified that a kind soul had been ruined there. Tormented souls lived within solitary trees, and people believed blood flowed within them instead of sap. Creaking trees likewise housed the souls of those in torment. If anyone dared to cut the tree down, the soul would be forced to find a new home. To discover whose soul lived within the tree was easy to accomplish by falling asleep beneath the tree and dreaming of the deceased. He could then converse with you and tell you how long he had been there and what sins from his life now tormented him. Additionally, if anyone picked a branch or fruit from a tree that grew in a cemetery, the soul of the person residing there would suffer and haunt the living person with insomnia.

Healing Abilities

Not only were trees considered magical, they were also respected for their healing properties, which included physical and mental issues. This was especially true of old trees that grew alone in a field or near a spring. Their leaves, bark, roots, flowers, and fruits all contributed to the well-being of humankind—and still do today.

It isn't only the byproducts of trees that have healing capacity. Trees themselves are believed to have an energy that provides healing. People prayed to the trees or merely

beseeched them for healing. Spoken words were not always needed. Leaning against the tree or placing your hands on the trunk created a connection. Other instances involved sitting beneath the tree to absorb its healing energy.

People passed on their illness to the tree, which they believed would scatter the disease to the wind through its branches or into the ground through its roots. The people did not merely take from the tree. In return for its help, people thanked the tree and left it gifts or sacrifices as payment for services the tree rendered. These gifts included food and drinks, towels, colorful ribbons, amulets, or a piece of the health seeker's clothing.

Various rituals involved healing a sick child while passing him through a hole in a tree. First, the trunk of a tree, often an oak, was split, and wedges were pounded into both sides of the trunk to keep it apart, so it formed a crevice. The parents or a healer and the mother would then pass the child through the hole to each other for a total of three times. As they did this, they prayed for the removal of the specific illness the child suffered or they said a charm like "Run away, wedges." They might also spit onto the ground.

The child's shirt was removed and placed within the crevice and the wedges removed. If the tree grew back together, they believed the child would recover. If the tree didn't regrow, the child was expected to die.

In a variation, the child was placed within the tree's fork while the parents walked around the tree either three or nine times. As the sick child passed through, it was believed he left his illness on the other side. At home, the child was bathed in water that had been gathered from nine rivers or wells. After that, the parent scattered ashes from seven furnaces over the child.

During a time of epidemic, all the village children could be brought to receive a tree's healing and protection. Two elderly women found a tree in which an animal had dug a hole around the roots. The women passed the children one at a time through the hole.

For adults, one method of healing was similar to the ritual of children being passed through the split trunk. Only the adult crawled three times through the roots of an oak or walnut that had been dug around.

Another ritual to get rid of fever or illness was to first bathe in a spring and dry oneself with a clean towel, thereby removing the illness with the cloth. The individual then transferred the illness to the tree by hanging the cloth on a branch. In both rituals, the sick person believed the illness would perish when the cloth decayed.

The ritual of passing through a tree was symbolic of rebirth. Often, the tree was old and sacred. This could be oak, beech, dogwood, or another associated with health and strength, because the tree was believed to pass on these characteristics to the ill person. Leaving the clothing in this case was not a gift to the tree, but a way to transmit the disease to the tree.

Not only do trees heal people, they also have the ability to heal their own kind. The more that is discovered about trees, the more awe-inspiring they become. It's come to light how a forest is a community, with trees taking care of one another. Through a fungal network, trees send electrical signals to warn others of danger. They provide a sugar solution nourishment

to each other through their intertwined root systems. Trees even send distress signals through the air by using pheromones and other scent signals. That sense of caring and protection even extends to the human race. People can tap into the energy of trees and find inner healing.

Bach's Thirty-eight Flowers

Each type of tree plays different roles and has different strengths. That is apparent in Bach's Thirty-eight Flowers. According to Dr. Edward Bach (1886–1936), herbal remedies from trees and other plants have been used to help with human emotions. In the 1930s, he prepared the first floral essences from thirty-eight flowers. He believed that physical symptoms were caused by emotional and mental conditions, and that the remedies he created from these flowers would restore balance caused by negative emotions.

These flowers are all non-toxic. Bach's Thirty-eight Flowers remedies are created from agrimony, aspen, beech, centaury, cerato, cherry plum, chestnut bud, chicory, clematis, crab apple, elm, gentian, gorse, heather, holly, honeysuckle, hornbeam, impatiens, larch,

mimulus, mustard, oak, olive, pine, red chestnut, rock rose, rock water, scleranthus, star of Bethlehem, sweet chestnut, vervain, vine, walnut, water violet, white chestnut, wild oat, wild rose, and willow. You'll find some of these floral remedies listed in this book.

Summary

People also often attribute human emotions to trees. The leaves of the aspen are said to quiver because of its shame in being the tree from which Judas Iscariot hanged himself. Another tale designates this tree as the birch, which turned white with fear because of the hanging. And yet another story says the birch forbid Judas from using it to kill himself. Birch is called capricious and capable of being offended and taking revenge on people who ask for help too often. And a Bulgarian proverb says, "The forest does not cry because of the axe but because of its handle," indicating that trees feel betrayal.

In poetry and folklore, attributing these human emotions to trees is acceptable. But do trees rationalize in this manner? Do they possess this type of intelligence? Are their actions conscious and intentional? Other scientists stick with more traditional, unemotional thinking and attribute tree behavior to natural selection.

Whether or not either view is completely or partially true is unimportant to this book. Trees are marvelous, majestic, and magical. You don't have to hug a tree to appreciate the value it brings to humankind.

The trees that follow are ones that have a special significance to Bulgarians. Some of these are ones that are included in the 77½ herbs we discussed in our book on that topic. Others are not part of that special ritual, but still play an important role in Bulgarian culture—either medicinally or magically.

MEDICAL LIABILITY DISCLAIMER: The information in this book and on our website is not intended to be medical advice, nor does it claim that the herbs listed are safe or effective to use in the manners described. It is not meant to diagnose, prevent, treat, or cure any disease. It is merely a brief summary of various herbal folk remedies and how they have been used in the past and may still be used today. We have not tried any of these remedies and cannot verify their effectiveness or safety. We accept no liability for the accuracy of the information. Some of the herbs listed here are partially or fully toxic, and may interact adversely and fatally with other medication. If you have any health concerns and wish to try herbal remedies, discuss the potential risks and benefits with a medical professional first.

MAGICAL DISCLAIMER: Magical ingredients and spells are for entertainment only. We have not tried any of these remedies, nor do we make any claims as to their effectiveness or safety.

SOURCES

Agapkina, Tatyana Alekseevna. "ДЕРЕВО, священные деревья как центр мира." [TREE, sacred trees as the center of the world.] http://www.bibliotekar.ru/2-9-3-slavyanskaya-mifologiya/101.htm.

Agapkina, Tatyana Alekseevna. "Деревья в славянской народной традиции: Очерки." [Trees in the Slavic folk tradition: Essays.] Indrik: Moscow, 2019. https://www.academia.edu/45107661/Деревья_в_славянской_народной_традиции_Очерки.

Agapkina, Tatyana Alekseevna and A. J. Toporkov. "Древнерусские Свидетельства О Почитании Деревьев." [Ancient Russian Evidence of the Veneration of Trees.] Leningrad Publishing House: Leningrad, 1988. http://www.bibliotekar.ru/2-9-10-volhvy-i-kolduny/20.htm.

Aleksstosich. "Стабло живота – The Tree of Life." September 27, 2018. https://svilenkonac.net/2018/09/27/стабло-живота-the-tree-of-life/.

Alvarez-Pedrosa, Juan Antonio, ed. Sources of Slavic Pre-Christian Religion. Brill: Leiden, Boston, 2021.

Aveela, Ronesa. A Study of Household Spirits of Eastern Europe. Bendideia Publishing: Swanzey, NH, 2018.

Aveela, Ronesa. Light Love Rituals: Bulgarian Myths, Legends, and Folklore. Bendideia Publishing: Swanzey, NH, 2014.

Baeva, Iskra. "The Holy Cross and its Feast." September 14, 2014. https://bnr.bg/en/post/100458571/the-holy-cross-and-its-feast.

B., Blagovesta. "The Oak tree worship in Slavic culture and its practice today." https://www.slavorum.org/the-oak-tree-worship-in-slavic-culture-and-its-practice-today/.

Grigorova, Darina. "Feast of the Cross at the Forest of the Cross." September 14, 2017. https://bnr.bg/post/100872970/feast-of-the-cross-at-the-forest-of-the-cross.

Malyuta, A. N. "Священные деревья древних славян." [Sacred trees of the ancient Slavs.] August 16, 2016. https://zvezdakrama.org/svyashhennye-derevya-drevnih-slavyan.

Markov, Al. "Krastova Gora - where faith in God banishes despondency." September 14, 2022. https://bnr.bg/en/post/101704742/krastova-gora-where-faith-in-god-banishes-despondency.

V., Stefan. "The Cult Of The Trees in Slavic Mythology." https://www.slavorum.org/the-cult-of-the-trees-in-slavic-mythology/.

SOURCES from *A Study of Dragons of Eastern Europe*

Aveela, Ronesa. *Light Love Rituals: Bulgarian Myths, Legends, and Folklore*. Bendideia Publishing: Swanzey, NH, 2014.

Georgieva, Ivanichka. *Bulgarian Mythology*. Sofia: Svyat Publishers, 1985.

Israfela. "How is the cosmos perceived according to the Bulgarian folk belief?" February 18, 2018. https://wiccanrede.org/2018/02/how-is-the-cosmos-perceived-according-to-the-bulgarian-folk-belief/.

Zhelev, Radostin. "The Golden Fruit Bearing Tree." March 9, 2012. https://bnr.bg/en/post/100144653/the-golden-fruit-bearing-tree.

The Soul of a Tree

A chapter from my memoir, A Tear and A Smile: Reflections of an Immigrant.

Have you ever wondered if trees have souls?

If you stand within a tree's shade, try pressing yourself to its bark to feel its heart pulsing and its leaves rustling like a whisper. Think about a centuries-old tree falling to the ground. The thunder is heard for hundreds of feet. Like a defeated giant after a long and heavy battle, the tree's body relaxes on the ground. Even though the tree itself has been destroyed, new shoots of sun-drenched branches emerge from its roots. It continues to grow as long as its roots are not extracted from the ground.

As a child, I imagined every tree as a person. The old walnut was a white-bearded old man with a wrinkled face; the pear was a huggable grandmother with her arms outstretched; the quince looked like a magnificent, smiling aunt; the willow danced like a ballerina to the whistling of the wind.

Trees are all around us. They are the lungs of the planet, filtering the air. In summer, they provide us cool shade from a sometimes-brutal sun. We enjoy their blossoms in spring and their beautiful colors in autumn. In winter we enjoy warmth from their wood in the fireplace. We use wooden implements to do housework, and wood to build our houses, schools, churches, iconostasis, art, and other objects used in everyday life.

In America, laws protect nature, ensuring our trees and forests are not completely wiped out. We can't stop all forests from being destroyed for their wood, but the law protects parks and nature reserves.

When we arrived in America twenty years ago, the plane landed in Boston. It was late in the evening and on our way to the home of our friends who would shelter us for the first few days, we saw only lights and silhouettes. The next morning my oldest daughter's laughter woke me. She was standing in her pajamas by the window, pointing outside with eyes wide open. When I looked, I was speechless. Several gray squirrels bounced from branch to branch in the crown of a huge tree covered with golden, orange, and red leaves, like an artist's palette. Some of the leaves had fallen onto a green carpet of well-cut grass. Green, trees, sun. Hypnotized, I went out barefoot and felt the dew on my soles. My daughters followed me. I felt like a child.

Was I dreaming? It felt surreal. It was an experience I will never forget. My first encounter with nature in an American suburb. We were in a town, one of many near Boston, with clean streets, green lawns, shrubs, and trees. Yes, as we saw it in Hollywood movies. But it didn't feel like a city. It was more like living in a remote hut on the top of a mountain.

After twenty years in America, I'm used to seeing greenery and trees. Large oaks surround our house and provide shade in summer and protection from the chilly winds in winter. In autumn, the leaves fall, and we complain that we need to collect them in sacks, but working outside helps us get closer to nature.

I love the whisper of the willows. We planted two beautiful weeping willows next to each other, like two sisters, reminding me of my children. Believe it or not, I grew them from two little shoots that I cut off the tree at my girls' school bus stop. The trees are more than twenty years old, growing up before our eyes in the same way our children did.

We planted a fir tree, and every Christmas we decorate it with lights. Santa Claus leaves presents there overnight year after year. The fir tree is already large, and every needle on the branches has recorded our beautiful memories.

In Bulgaria, my grandfather invested his money in land and forests. After 1941, the Communist Party confiscated all his estates and destroyed the forests without his permission. The division and distribution of forests is still a burning topic, and people continue to be killed for property. Unfortunately, the destruction of forests in Bulgaria continues today without planting new ones to replace them.

Everything in nature has its place. The destruction of forests affects not only bees, birds, and all its inhabitants, but also the waters. The network of tree roots protects riverbanks like natural levees. It's no wonder floods and mudslides dump houses and people down cliffs when trees along the rivers have all been chopped down.

Years ago in Sofia, chestnut trees lined the middle of the streets and the parks. The scent of white flowers filled the capital, and the greenery cooled the asphalt from the burning rays of the summer sun. Golden leaves covered the streets during autumn. Over the years, the city grew, the number of cars increased, streets widened, and the chestnuts lost the fight against asphalt. The last time I visited my mother, I heard that illness and small parasites threatened to destroy the surviving chestnuts. And other trees could be ruined as well if the disease continues to spread and no one cares about the green areas of the city. Asphalt, cars, and dust cover the narrow streets instead of the beauty of trees.

They say you need a whole village to raise a child, but the same can be said of a tree. It's hard to grow a tree. It's like a human. It needs to find the right place and the correct soil to grow healthy and happy.

I read an article about palm trees in Ecuador that are moving to find light, water, and good soil. They grow new roots that reach the water and let the old die, allowing them to move and reach good soil and light. Interesting, right? This is like humans. We're looking for a better life and livelihood, and so we travel, we wander, from place to place.

Unfortunately, the destruction of forests isn't a phenomenon only in Bulgaria; it happens all over the world. I'm glad when I see news about people planting trees, trying to recover the destroyed treasure and help the planet breathe.

The most common mythical symbol of the universe is the "World Tree." Its separate parts symbolize the three layers of the world. The crown symbolizes the heavens—God, the saints, and the angels live there. The stem represents earthly life, and the roots the underworld. The tree is woven as a motif in Bulgarian rug patterns, embroidery, and wedding rituals.

The tree for many people and nations is a symbol of the connection between the earth and the sky. With roots deep in the soil and branches bending toward the sun. Almost all the ancient nations worshiped the tree—real or idealized. It was attributed to the cosmic symbols. According to ancient religions, trees are living creatures; they're inhabited by spirits of nature, nymphs, and elves. Every tree has its own soul. And every tree has its owner or dragon (*zmey*).

Sacred places in villages called *obroks* are scattered under branches of centuries-old trees. They're found near springs, places where the whole village gathers to celebrate, perform sacrifices, and honor the soul of the tree. The centuries-old trees and obrok require special tribute, in the same way chapels, churches, and monasteries do. People believe that praying to the tree and the creature within it will keep the village safe from evil forces and will bring fertility and prosperity to the land and people. Normally in these sacred places, you see stone slabs or stone crosses. Sometimes people drill holes in the tree, pour in oil and other offerings, and cover the hole with wax to feed the spirits.

In my grandparents' village, there are several old obroks. One of them is for St. George. It's at the highest and most beautiful part of the village. The church was built near the obrok in the early twentieth century. Both are places for the villagers to pay respect to the saint.

These sacred places are created under oak, beech, and other centuries-old trees. Bulgarians usually think of oak, maple, walnut, and pine as World Trees. The mythology of the mountain people retains pre-Christian beliefs, according to which the world is a great oak tree. The image of an oak and an eagle on the top is a prototype of the World Tree and is found in legends, tales, and stories and in traditional songs of the people of northern Bulgaria, where my ancestors are from. This image also occurs on iconostasis carvings and thrones in the churches. These eagles are believed to be the guardians against hail, and they protect fields from fire and *lamia*, an evil dragon. The oak is also a road between the upper and the lower land, our world and the underworld.

Tradition has strictly forbidden people from even chopping their branches. The old ones believe that if you cut down such a tree, you and your family will be cursed, and you'll get sick and die because a saint is sitting inside it.

It sounds ridiculous, but I think my father who left this world suddenly at an early age may have broken this rule and paid with his life. He cared for his family, worked a lot, had many talents, and built a house, not only one, but a few houses. He was building one for a grandmother whose old home the Communist had destroyed. However, an old walnut, with towering branches and heavily rooted in the ground, proudly sat near the foundation, hindering the construction of the home. On the ninth of September, my father decided to cut it down. I don't remember the year. I think it was 1981 or 1982, but I'm certain it was September 9.

How do I remember the date? On the ninth of September every year, there was music in the center of the village, people commemorating the Communist Party's anniversary. The tree was a few yards from the square, and the mayor came personally to stop the cutting of the tree, because the noise was interfering with the holiday. My father ignored him, and after a few hours, the old giant crashed down.

My father used the walnut wood to make windows, doors, and other things for the new house. The boards had unique patterns and colors. Because of these features of walnut, iconostases in churches are made of this wood. My father continued the construction of the house, but after a couple of years, he died suddenly on his fiftieth birthday, unable to see the completed fruit of his labor. I always think that the saint or the spirit who was living in the walnut tree took his spirit with him. The old walnut's soul is built into the house, and every time I go there, I can feel it.

If trees had voices, think about what they could tell us: what they saw and heard over hundreds of years. In Luti Dol in Bulgaria, my grandmother's village, there's a cheshma and a small creek called Bivola. Nearby is a willow people say is more than 500 years old. I always wondered what the tree saw during those 500 years. Along the spring runs the old road to Sofia. Maybe the tree saw the rise and fall of the Turks, the lines of families rushing to get out to save their lives during the wars.

Gold and treasure gathered from the sweat and misery of the people once was transported over this road. Maybe the tree saw German and Russian soldiers in 1944. Every time I went to the spring with my grandmother, I always touched the tree's trunk in the hope of hearing its voice, waiting to hear its story.

The village has an old legend from 1765 that its inhabitants pass on mouth-to-mouth. One summer morning, a group of youths who were hunting in the woods saw a strange woman on one of the hills around the village. She had a terribly ugly face, a bony body, and long, shaggy hair. She drew a big bow, and with malice began to send blazing arrows toward the village. All the young people who lived there were struck by a terrible disease. The old men in the village gathered together, wondering what this curse was and how to save the people, but it was too late. One of the elders told them that it was Mora, the horrible plague. The disease spread like fire and destroyed almost the entire village. Fear, weeping, and the smell of death passed through the empty streets. The people who escaped from the village were overtaken by the arrows of the disease, and hundreds of bodies covered the surrounding meadows and forests near the village. Not many people survived the plague, but those who did were able to rebuild, and the area was named "Dead Meadows" as a reminder of the event and the people who died.

Everyone believes in something that brings hope and peace to their soul. For millennia, people have believed in mythical beings, deities, and holy trees; others believe in the power of crystals. All of this helps us to not fear the uncertainty of life and to predict the course of events in our lives. Our life is like a chapter of a book that has no end. Everyone writes their chapter to leave a trace behind them.

I always wanted the ability to talk to trees. I can learn so much from them.

FIELD MAPLE

Acer campestre

Acer campestre
Field maple

Bright green leaves form on long stalks in opposite pairs along the stem. As they unfold, they become darker. The leaves are composed of five round lobes with smooth edges. In autumn, the leaves turn bright yellow or golden yellow and may have a red tinge.

Small insignificant yellowish-green flowers bud in clusters at around the same time the leaves appear. They produce a dry green, pink-tinted fruit called a samara, which has two one-seeded cells surrounded by wings, which spin as they fall. These divide when they ripen, and can be transported quite far by the wind.

The trunk, branches, and leaves all produce a saccharine juice, and the sap drawn from the tree contains sugar.

History and Traditions: The origin of the genus name is uncertain, but it may come from the Proto-Indo-European *ak-* for "be sharp," referring to the fact the wood was hard and was used to make spears. The specific name comes from the Latin *campus* for "of the fields" or "of the plains."

A popular tradition among children is to wear the split samara on the bridge of their noses. An older tradition in nineteenth century Great Britain was to pass a child through the branches of a maple tree. This removed any witchcraft that was making the child ill and ensured he remained healthy for many years. And hanging maple branches around a doorway was believed to keep bats from entering. Maple utensils were also thought to hold magical powers. Anyone who ate with a maple spoon would not be troubled by magic, and if the person happened to eat poisoned food with a maple utensil, he would not be harmed.

The first thing that comes to my mind when I think about the maple tree is the sticky sap that's made into a sweet syrup that many love to pour over pancakes. If you live in the New England area, you'll likely have bought Vermont maple syrup. Besides being a delightful treat, maple syrup represents success and abundance.

Description: This maple grows to a height of 50 to 85 feet (15 to 25 meters), while in some locations it may only reach of height of 25 to 35 feet (8 to 10 meters) and can be pruned to form a tall hedge. The light gray bark is smooth and finely cracked. As the tree ages, the bark peels away in small scales. The crown is low, domed, compact, and bushy, with short lateral shoots, and has a spread of 25 to 35 feet (8 to 10 meters).

CAUTION: No known hazards, but always consult with a medical professional before using herbs medicinally. Pregnant and lactating women should avoid use due to lack of information on its safety.

Perhaps the most popular symbol of the maple is the leaf proudly displayed in the middle of the Canadian flag, which symbolizes Canadian sacrifice during World War I. The flag was approved in December of 1964, and on February 15, 1965, it became official through royal proclamation. Even before this, the maple leaf has been a national symbol in Canada since 1868, symbolizing pride and strength.

Habitat and Distribution: This maple variety is native to Europe and western Asia, and the trees can be found on plains, hills, and along rivers. It has been introduced to parts of the U.S. and western Australia.

Growth: Deciduous tree. Flowers bloom between April and June, depending on the location, and seeds ripen in September and October. The tree prefers full sun to partial shade, although in its early life, it's resistant to shade, only requiring increased light as it ages and starts producing seeds.

A maple prefers warmer weather, but can also tolerate severe winters and is resistant to frost. The tree can withstand strong winds, but not a marine exposure. It can tolerate air pollution and droughts. The tree grows best with a medium amount of water that keeps the soil moist, but it can adapt to various soil types, including heavy clay.

The tree is not one that first grows in a newly disturbed area as its seeds lie dormant under vegetation for twelve to eighteen months. Once the seedlings become well-established, at five to eight years, they will begin a more rapid growth for about twenty-five years.

Harvesting: The bark of young twigs is used for medicinal purposes. It should be dried in the sun and stored in a dry place.

Medical Use: Maple is a diuretic and astringent. It also has been used as a remedy for vomiting, jaundice, kidney stones, gout, and wounds. A decoction of the bark is used to wash sore eyes. To take internally, pour 500 ml of boiling water over 3 teaspoons of crushed bark. Let it soak until it cools,

---

Honey-Dew Rain

If you've ever walked beneath a maple, you may have felt drops like a fine rain. This is because the tree is likely infected with aphids, and the "rain" you experience is produced by the insects. The aphids eat holes in the leaves and suck out the juices, then proceed to excrete drops of sticky honey-dew every half hour. With numerous insects eating the leaves above you, many drops will fall from the tree (Botanical.com).

then strain out the bark. Take 1 Tablespoon several times a day. You can also use this solution when you wash your hair to prevent hair loss.

Rituals and Magical Use: Maple is a peaceful wood. Wands made from the tree have been used for spiritual healing, and spells about art, beauty, binding, and abundance should include the wood. If it's love you're looking for, try eating the seeds to draw love to yourself, since maple enables you to look for a companion who is strong, devoted, and cares for others. Or if money is your forte, include maple as a base in loose incense, and you may find it brings you gold. The tree is one of balance. It shows you options, so you can make a good choice, and you can use maple for divination. Not least of all, maple helps you gain knowledge and enhances intellectual pursuits.

When people wanted to heal a child, for example, from a hernia, they mentioned maple in the ritual, because they believed the tree was insensitive to pain. A ritual healing involved first measuring the ill child on a window jamb. Then, they drilled a hole into the wood at the child's height and drove in a maple peg. As they did this, they said, "Just as a maple tree doesn't feel anything and doesn't know about the wind or weather, so too, the servant of God has a hernia that doesn't hurt and is unaffected by the wind and the weather."

Ancient Slavs believed that people could be turned into maples, and you could tell this because the maple leaf's five lobes resemble the human hand. In one story, a mother cursed her misbehaving son to become a maple. A musician made a violin from the tree, and the boy's voice sang from the instrument and told a tale about his mother. Another belief was that a *kaval* (similar to a flute) or whistle made from the maple's wood would tell tales about a ruined life.

The tree itself has magical properties. Many a person out in the woods has found shelter under the maple's branches. Unlike the shadow of the walnut tree, which steals power from anyone who sleeps within it, the maple's shadow is a source of positive energy. Sleeping under the tree guarantees one peace and protection from mythical creatures like the Bulgarian nymphs called Samodivi, who roam the forest.

Even objects made from maple wood offer this protection. A shepherd will dare to play his kaval while tending his sheep if the musical instrument has been made from maple. If it's made of other wood, he may not be so lucky. This is because Samodivi love the music and will force a shepherd to play all night long while they dance beneath the moon. The next morning, if the poor man hasn't died of exhaustion, he'll discover that he's worn holes in the ground from tapping his feet to his own music.

Additionally, when Rusalki (often called mermaids) come out, magical healers called *rusalii* or *kalushari* chase the maidens away with sticks made of maple, hazel, or dogwood.

Within the household, important objects were made from wood in order to provide protection from black magic and all manner of bad things. In particular, maple was chosen for objects used to hold or convey liquids, such as buckets or brandy and wine flasks, as well as a rocker arm used to carry water. It was a popular belief that malicious spirits resided within water, and so they would flee when coming in contact with maple.

Vampires were among the spirits, or undead, affected by this. The Slavs held many beliefs about how a person could become a vampire: a cat or other animal leaping over the corpse or a bird flying above the body could trigger the curse. One method of protecting a deceased loved one from becoming a vampire was to make his coffin from maple or pine. On top of that, grasses and herbs blessed on the Feast of the Transfiguration were laid inside the coffin.

If these precautions were not taken, the vampire could be destroyed by the ever-popular stake through the heart. The stabber had to make sure the stake was maple, ash, or hawthorn in order for it to be effective.

Other Use: Although the sugar concentration in this type of maple is lower than in sugar maples, its juice can be used as a beverage or made into a syrup or sweetener. Maple leaves wrapped around apples, roots, and so on are an excellent way to preserve them.

Maples can be pruned to make hedges, and they are attractive ornamental plants, as well as lovely additions to floral decorations. This maple variety is suited to making bonsai trees, due to its growth habits and small leaves. Its root system is good for lessening soil erosion.

Maple wood is compact and has a fine grain, with beautiful veins, enhanced by polish, making the wood suitable for cabinets, furniture, flooring, violin cases, as well as bowls, cups, and other kitchenware. It's also a good wood for fuel. The young shoots were once used as whips since they were flexible and tough.

Other Names: Common maple, hedge maple, dog oak, common elder, master tree.

Aromatic: The sap produced is sticky and sweet.

SOURCES

Agapkina, Tatyana Alekseevna. "Деревья в славянской народной традиции: Очерки." [Trees in the Slavic folk tradition: Essays.] Indrik: Moscow, 2019. https://www.academia.edu/45107661/Деревья_в_ славянской_народной_традиции_Очерки.

Bezovska, Albena. "Bulgarian folk beliefs and customs on Spasovden." May 28, 2020. https://bnr.bg/en/post/ 101283395/bulgarian-folk-beliefs-and-customs-on-spasovden.

Botanical.com. "Maples." https://botanical.com/botanical/mgmh/m/maples14.html.

Chernikova, Kristina. "Клен." [Maple.] https://gotvach.bg/n-44730-Клен.

Etymonline.com. "Acer (n.)." https://www.etymonline.com/search?q=Acer+campestre.

Framar.bg. "Клен, Полски клен." [Maple, Field maple.] April 16, 2010, updated on March 2, 2022. https://medpedia.framar.bg/ботаника/клен.

Isabella. "The Magickal Maple Tree." December 9, 2017. https://speakingofwitchwands.net/2017/09/12/the-magickal-maple-tree/.

Konstantinova, Daniela. "Trees that Bulgarians venerate most." December 26, 2015. https://bnr.bg/en/post/100635118/trees-that-bulgarians-venerate-most.

Kubijovyč, Volodymyr, ed. *Ukraine, a Concise Encyclopedia*. University of Toronto Press: Toronto, 1963. https://hdl.handle.net/2027/iau.31858049887304.

Máchal, Jan. "Slavic." In *The Mythology of All the Races*, vol. 3, edited by Herbert Louis Gray with consulting editor George Foot Moore, 217-330. Boston: Marshall Jones Company, 1918. https://hdl.handle.net/2027/nyp.33433068186265.

Malyuta, A. N. "Священные деревья древних славян." [Sacred trees of the ancient Slavs.] August 16, 2016. https://zvezdakrama.org/svyashhennye-derevya-drevnih-slavyan.

Markov, Alexander, trans. "Forests in Bulgarian Folklore." April 7, 2010. https://bnr.bg/en/post/100104832/forests-in-bulgarian-folklore.

Missouri Botanical Garden. "Acer campestre." https://www.missouribotanicalgarden.org/PlantFinder/PlantFinderDetails.aspx?taxonid=275376.

Ralston, William Ralston Shedden. *Russian Folk-tales*. London: Smith, Elder & Co., 1873. https://hdl.handle.net/2027/uc1.31158010565728.

Smith, Whitney. "Flag of Canada." Last Updated: Nov 28, 2022. https://www.britannica.com/topic/flag-of-Canada.

Woodland Trust. "Maple, field." https://www.woodlandtrust.org.uk/trees-woods-and-wildlife/british-trees/a-z-of-british-trees/field-maple/.

SILVER BIRCH
Betula pendula

Betula pendula **Silver birch**

⚠️

The triangular-shaped leaves are coarse and double-toothed. In autumn, they turn from glossy-green to yellow.

The silver birch bears catkins, small, slim, cylindrical flowers that form in clusters. Males are yellowish-brown and drooping, while females are greenish and upright. They produce conelike fruits that contain many small winged seeds.

History and Traditions: The genus name is Latin for "birch," and the specific name comes from the Latin *pendere* for "to hang." The word "birch" derives from the Proto-Indo-European root *bhereg-*, which means "to shine, bright, white." This definition appropriately defines the silver birch's bark, which is bright white with black fissures. *Betula pendula* is often confused with the similar *Betula alba* (white birch), whose bark is a grayer color.

Birch is called a pioneer species, because it's often one of the first plants to re-grow in fire-ravaged locations and has been said to be among those that first repopulated rocky land when Ice-Age glaciers receded.

The tree has an important role in many cultures. In Slavic folklore, it's the tree of sorrow and new life. Ancient Romans, among others, worshipped the sacred tree as a goddess. During Samhain, Celts drove away the spirits of the old year with birch twigs. Other cultures thought of birch as the tree of the dead.

Birch tar was once used in the making of leather and as a lubricant. And in the early part of the twentieth century, the French used birch tar to create a perfume called "Russian leather."

Birch has always been one of my favorite trees. It fascinated me to peel the curling bark when I was a child. The tree's white color stands out in a forest of grays and browns. Birch appears delicate and dainty compared to the more powerful trees like oak and elm. To me, birch always said, "Admire me. I'm different." It's no wonder the tree is called the "Lady of the Forest" in Russian folklore and is associated with the Great Goddess.

Description: The silver birch grows around 82 feet (25 meters) tall and spreads to around 15 to 30 feet (4.5 to 9 meters). Its crown is pyramidal to oval shaped. The tree's white, thin, papery bark peels off in layers, and its tender shoots are bumpy. As the tree matures, it becomes furrowed and blackish-gray near its base.

CAUTION: Children or pregnant or lactating women should not use. Birch products can also hurt kidneys and irritate dry skin.

Habitat and Distribution: Native to Europe and Asia and introduced to North America. The tree is often found on mountains and along hills, crags, and the edges of forests. In Bulgaria, you can find it in forests at the base of foothills.

Growth: Deciduous tree. The flowers blossom in March and April, and the fruits mature in late summer. The plant thrives in cool climates but requires plenty of sunlight and afternoon shade. It has shallow roots, so it needs moist soil that is well-drained, but can tolerate some dry soils. It can thrive in sandy or rocky loam.

Harvesting: Buds, leaves, and bark are used. Leaf buds are collected in April and May before they burst. Cut the buds along with the twigs. Dry them in a well-ventilated area or in a dehydrator at 86°F (30°C). When dry, break off the twigs. Leaves are harvested in spring, both before the tree flowers and afterward, when they have fully developed, around April to June. Dry them in the shade or in a dehydrator at the same temperature as the buds. Peel off the bark in early spring when the juices start to flow. All of its products should be stored in dry, ventilated areas.

Medical Use: Substances in birch bark have anti-inflammatory, antiviral, and anti-cancer properties and are being studied by medical professionals for possible treatment.

In folk medicine, components of birch are remedies for many ailments, such as improving metabolism, lowering blood pressure, and reducing cholesterol. The leaves and sap help dissolve kidney stones, but this remedy also irritates the kidneys, so use it only under professional medical supervision.

Ointments made from the sap treat skin problems (eczema, warts, psoriasis) but are likely to irritate dry skin. The bark, applied externally, is believed to ease muscle pain. Birch has also been used for rheumatism, gout, and leprosy.

People drink an infusion made from young birch leaves to treat things such as nervous disorders and colic, and drink it as a stimulant, anti-inflammatory agent, antiseptic, and for vitamins.

Rituals and Magical Use: Birch, in particular a twisted or crooked tree, is a favorite of the Slavic water spirits called Rusalki. They love to sit within its branches. A straight, tall birch was more likely to attract benevolent spirits like the Bereginya, from whom the birch gets its Russian name of *beryoza*. April 11, Bereshchenye, is considered the tree's birthday. It wakes up on this day and allows its juices to flow.

A Slavic holiday associated with birch is Semik (Trinity), celebrated in June. People decorate their homes with garlands made from birch, and they hang decorations on the trees for the forest spirits. During this celebration, young women of marriageable age go into the woods to perform a "curling of the birch" ritual. They look for a birch sapling that's beginning to leaf and decorate it with ribbons, beads, cloth, thread, garlands, and other adornments. Then the women knot and twist the ends of the branches to form circles, symbolic of infinity, and dance around the tree while they sing. If the tree is at the edge of the forest close to the planted fields, the girls bend its tip and tie it to the ground. Since the birch is the first to foliate, it has "sacred energy" and "power of vegetation." Performing this action allows the tree to return this energy and life-giving moisture to the soil so it can be transferred to the grain fields.

Other spirits connected with birch are Leshy (forest spirit) and Vodyanoy (water spirit). When ancient Slavs entered the forest or traveled by the river, they would write a message to these spirits. It could be to help hunters capture game, or to beseech the spirits to return lost animals, or even to protect the traveler from harm.

Birch is used for divination. Young women weave the branches together into a braid and leave it alone overnight. If the braid has come undone in the morning when they check on it, it means the woman will get married that year. This represents a wedding custom where the bride's single braid is undone and re-braided into two, signifying her and her husband. Another way to forecast a potential wedding is to toss a floral crown onto a birch. If it doesn't fall off, the woman will get married that year. A more ominous custom is to throw birch crowns into a river. A sinking crown means death, one that returns to the bank indicates a future marriage, and if it floats away, it is a sign the girl will marry soon.

Since it is one of the first plants to come into leaf in spring, birch is symbolic of purification, innocence, and renewal of life as nature awakens. And in many cultures, it represents motherhood. Pregnant women asked birch to give them strength and make their labor easy. Many traditions use birch to ensure health, love, and happiness for those with new

---

Daughters of Adam

Birch trees are associated with the feminine, in particular murdered women, with the girls either becoming a birch upon their death or a tree grew over their grave. It was a favorite tree for young women and married ones to tell their joys and sorrows.

Another legend says that birch trees were once the daughters of Adam. Their long braids grew into the ground, and they became trees, and the juice they weep is their tears. They became white with fear because of Judas Iscariot and forbid him from hanging himself on their branches (Stanton).

Birch Sap for Wellness

It's commonly believed that the sap from a birch has the greatest healing power in early May. People collected it until the twelfth of the month. Those who were ill or sick drank it to become healthier. However, people didn't want to overtax any one tree, believing it became exhausted if they took more than 1 liter of the sap. Once harvesters gathered the sap, they covered the tree's wound and thanked the tree for aiding them. This same tree would be left alone for a year afterward, neither taking more sap nor cutting its branches, so it could fully recover (Czarnik).

beginnings, such as births, weddings, and new home constructions.

Various folk beliefs about birch come from its white color. On one hand, it symbolizes purity. The evil eye cannot stick to the tree. Also, from Palm Sunday until Easter, only a birch broom can be used to sweep out homes. This is because it is the only one that can sweep out the evil spirits. On the other hand, the birch's white color is like milk, and therefore can be a witch's tool. She "milks" the tree as a way to steal milk from a cow.

Birch is made into a dousing rod to find minerals, buried treasure, and water. People also believed that having a branch under the roof or in the attic protected the home from lightning and hail. In addition, they placed the branches among the crops to drive away birds and rodents, as well as provide for an abundant harvest.

Birch is a healing tree. It was a common belief that birch energizes people and can prolong youth and slow aging. But the tree the sap was collected from couldn't be too old; it had to be between seven and fifty years old. Whipping a sick person with a birch twig was meant to drive the illness out, and shaking the tree with the words "Shake me like I shake you, and then let go of me" would dispel the illness. Also, the twigs above the sick person were twisted, and the tree was threatened that they wouldn't be let go until the illness left the sick person. Additionally, a child's disease could be transferred to the tree by pouring bath water onto the roots while reciting a charm that included the person's name and illness they wanted to "throw under the birch bush."

Merely being near a birch tree can make a sick person feel better as well. It works not only for one's physical health, but for mental well-being also. Vulnerable people meditate by or communicate with a birch when they have difficulty assessing their life to strengthen their self-esteem. This works also to relieve depression, fatigue, and stress.

Birch protects people from physical and spiritual misfortunes. Its newly sprouted twigs are strong talismans that can not only cure diseases, but also break spells. People put babies in swings made of birch to protect the infants from evil charms. Having a birch grow near your home is welcome, because it will chase away nightmares. But since birch is also considered capricious, Slavs tended to plant them by the gate, rather than close to the house. By the gate, it would keep trouble from entering the home.

When a Siberian shaman is ready to begin a spiritual journey, he may climb to the top of a birch to put him closer to the upper realm.

Other Use: Sap from the tree is made into a drink, similar to the process of extracting sap from maples.

Ground birch bark was once a food staple in Sweden for making bread during famines.

In Finnish saunas, fragrant birch twigs are used to beat the bather's body lightly. Other homestead uses for the wood are to make furniture, plywood, skis, window frames, broom handles, kitchen utensils, and more, and bast shoes from the bark.

Birch is also used for toiletry items. An extract from birch is found in bath oils, face creams, shampoos, perfumes, soap, and shaving creams.

Because of birch's appearance, the bark is applied decoratively to floral bouquets. You can also make lovely Christmas candle holders from the wood—to either keep or give away.

Other Names: European white birch, East Asian white birch, warty birch, common birch, lady birch, lady of the woods, weeping birch.

Aromatic: Ground leaf buds have a pleasant aroma but tart taste. The leaves have no smell and are slightly bitter. The bark also lacks an odor and is bitter. The processed birch tar, however, is an oily liquid that has a smoke and leather aroma.

SOURCES

Agapkina, Tatyana Alekseevna. "Деревья в славянской народной традиции: Очерки." [Trees in the Slavic folk tradition: Essays.] Indrik: Moscow, 2019. https://www.academia.edu/45107661/Деревья_в_ славянской_народной_традиции_Очерки.

Aveela, Ronesa. *A Study of Rusalki – Slavic Mermaid of Eastern Europe*. Bendideia Publishing: Swanzey, NH, 2019.

Czarnik, Phoenix. "Birch Bark Charming." September 21, 2021. https://www.facebook.com/groups/ 58602598939/posts/10158581955608940/. Original from https://stazip.ru.

Field, Jana. "Tree Symbolism: 8 Trees and Their Spiritual Meanings." June 3, 2022. https://www.journeytreehealing.com/post/tree-symbolism-8-trees-and-their-spiritual-meanings.

G., Jeanne. "Брезата пази от негативна енергия и депресия." [Birch protects against negative energy and depression.] https://sanovnik.bg/n4-6088-Брезата_пази_от_негативна_енергия_и_депресия.

Ivanov, Ivan Isaev, Prof.; Iliya Ivanov Landzhev, Dr. of Pharmacy; Geo Kirilov Neshev, Dr. of Medicine. *Билките в България и използването им.* [Herbs in Bulgaria and their use.] Zemizdat: Sofia, 1977.

Missouri Botanical Garden. "Betula pendula." http://www.missouribotanicalgarden.org/PlantFinder/ PlantFinderDetails.aspx?taxonid=277818&isprofile=1&basic=Betula%20pendula.

Petrova, Bilyana, Dr. "Бяла бреза, Метлика, Чупла, Ясика." [White birch, Metlika, Chupla, Yasika.] March 18, 2010, updated on January 7, 2021. https://medpedia.framar.bg/ботаника/бяла-бреза-метлика-чупла-ясика.

Stanton, Olga. "Sacred Trees of Slavs: Birch." April 12, 2021. https://www.facebook.com/slavicmagpie/posts/ pfbid032YfkcAWAL7bc9tESSdaTheUoThyFfDv8Aj91QgwpjwbxS7U2jntanBoLzs5odGNRl.

StunPeace. "МАГИЧЕСКАТА СИЛА НА БРЕЗАТА." [The magical power of the birch.] March 7, 2012. http://dobreedaznaete.blogspot.com/2012/03/blog-post_07.html.

Trees for Life. "Birch mythology and folklore." https://treesforlife.org.uk/into-the-forest/trees-plants-animals/trees/birch/birch-mythology-and-folklore/.

CHESTNUT
Castanea sativa

Castanea sativa
Chestnut

⚠️

Chestnuts are a popular autumn food, evoking images of the nuts roasting over an open fire. The warm, sweet scent permeates the air and fills passers-by with all the traditional holiday spirit that goes along with the season. The tree's flowers and nuts make lovely decorations, the wood is durable, and the trees can live for a couple thousand years.

Description: A mature tree stands at a height of around 80 to 100 feet (25 to 30 meters). It has a spread of about 30 to 50 feet (9 to 15 meters), with a crown shape described as pyramidal-rounded to broad columnar.

The tree's bark is purplish gray and smooth when it's young. As the tree ages, deep fissures develop in a spiral shape along the entire trunk. Older trees tend to develop shoots along the trunk, making its shape irregular.

Oblong-lanceolate leaves are slightly furry and are dark green on top and lighter on the underside. They are coarse-toothed with numerous prominent parallel veins. In autumn, the leaves turn yellow.

Yellowish-green catkins produce tiny flowers that are densely clustered. The flowers on the mid to upper portions are male, while a smaller number of females bloom at the base of the catkin. The males and females of a single tree do not pollinate themselves, but require pollination from nearby chestnut trees.

Female flowers that do become pollinated produce prickly husks which hold three to seven fruits, brown nuts with a pointed tip. Cultivated trees contain only a single kernel. These have two skins. The outer one is brown and shiny, while the internal skin adheres to a creamy white center.

CAUTION: Pregnant and lactating women should avoid medicinal use of chestnuts since not enough is known about possible negative effects. For everyone else, chestnut products seem safe taken orally, but there is insufficient information about their safety as a skin medication. Eating raw chestnuts may cause stomach irritation, nausea, or liver damage for those who have liver disease or kidney problems.

History and Traditions: The Latin genus name comes from the Greek *kastaneia* for "nut from Castanea" or "nut from Castana," and the specific name means it's sown or cultivated by humans, instead of being produced in the wild. The common name of chestnut comes from the Old French *chastain* and the Middle English *chasteine*, which in time became *chesten nut*. In British slang, "old chestnut" means an old joke or story.

For thousands of years, chestnuts have been a food source, particularly for the poor. During certain eras, however, large cultivated nuts were considered luxury items. Roman soldiers ate a chestnut porridge before they went into battle.

A "chestnut civilization" arose in marginal and mountainous regions where wheat production didn't exist. Here, chestnuts were not only a food staple, but were part of the lives and traditions of the communities and essential to the populace's survival. The first unambiguous evidence of this type of civilization dates back to 2100–2050 B.C.) and was discovered in regions of Anatolia, northeastern Greece, and southeastern Bulgaria.

The Little Ice Age and the spread of crops of maize and potatoes, along with the Industrial Revolution, brought a decline to the "golden age" of chestnuts.

Habitat and Distribution: Native to temperate forest areas of southeastern Europe and southwestern Asia.

Growth: Deciduous tree. Flowers bloom in early to mid-summer, and the nuts fall during autumn. Seed-

---

Old Recipe for Stomachache

In the twelfth century, German abbess and physician Hildegard von Bingen (1098–1179) recorded a recipe for stomachache. It consisted of a chestnut puree made from 3 to 5 chestnuts, 3 spoonsful of spelt flour, 1.5 spoonsful of licorice, and 1 spoonful of polypody powder (Kosňovská, 173).

A Prickly Beauty

The god Jupiter was at it again, desiring a beautiful nymph. This time her name was Caste Nea (Chaste Néa), and she was a servant of the goddess Diana. The nymph had no desire to be another conquest of the gods, and so she spurned Jupiter. She preferred to lose her life over her virtue. Of course, Jupiter was furious, and he changed her into a chestnut tree. Her thorny burs were forever to remind her that she would have a painful destiny (Kosňovská, 66).

First, remove the outer prickly shell from the fruit. To use them for sowing the following year, you'll want to store them in a cool, shady location until the surface moisture has evaporated. Then store the chestnuts at low temperatures, but not below 32°F (0°C).

For consumption use, you can store chestnuts for a few months between layers of fine dry sand inside a wooden container in a cool, dry place. Clean, wash, and thoroughly dry fresh chestnuts. Then store them in a refrigerator for a month at a temperature of 35 to 37°F (2 to 3°C), or in a freezer in food-grade storage bags for up to six months. If you've boiled them or roasted them, let them cool before storing in the refrigerator for a few days or longer in the freezer.

You can also dry shelled chestnuts in a dehydrator at 100°F (38°C) for a couple of days, while unshelled ones require three days. Store the nuts for up to two months. When using them, first soak them in water overnight.

Medical Use: Chestnuts are a healthy snack, being low in fat and high in vitamin C. They are also a good source of fiber (improving digestion and balancing blood sugar) and antioxidants (reducing the risk of cardiovascular problems). To avoid the nuts losing vitamin C while they're cooking, roast them at a low temperature or dry them in a dehydrator.

Experiments with chestnuts have produced other surprising remedies. An extract from the nut, along with arnica and lemon oil, has been combined with mud from the salty lakes near Burgas, Bulgaria, to produce a treatment for varicose veins.

And speaking of mud, spas in Bulgaria offer what they call a sun-and-chestnut therapy. The chestnuts used are taken from trees that grow near a children's playground. The spa claims the nuts absorb both the sun's rays and the positively charged energy produced in the playground, and so impart this energy to those who undergo the spa treatment.

grown trees bear fruit after about twenty years, while grafted trees may take only five years.

The tree requires full sun, with six hours of sunlight daily, but it can tolerate moderate shade. Insufficient sunlight causes the tree's branches to become slender and fragile, and possibly unable to hold the weight of the blossoms and fruit. A chestnut tree prefers moist, well-drained loamy or sandy soils, but doesn't tolerate lime or clay soil. Once established, the tree is drought resistant, but is sensitive to frost.

Harvesting: Leaves, bark, and fruits are used. The leaves and bark should be collected in June or July; they can be used fresh or dried. The fruits are harvested around October after they fall from the tree. To make the fruits plump and concentrate the nutrients, keep only the early blossoms and trim the rest.

Other treatments using chestnut include breathing problems like bronchitis and whooping cough; digestive problems that cause diarrhea and bloody stool; plus weight gain, bladder problems, headaches, and depression. Tannins in the nut help reduce swelling.

Sweet chestnut is one of the elixirs created from Bach's Thirty-eight Flowers, which use non-poisonous plants and are geared toward restoring balance. This remedy, made from white chestnut blossoms, is called the "Flower of Liberation" and is meant for those suffering from unbearable depression with no hope of finding a way to beat it. Everything the sufferer has tried has failed, leaving him in utter despair. He believes everyone has forgotten him, and all he experiences is darkness, despair, and isolation. As Bach says, it's used "when the mind or body seems to have reached the limits of tolerance and only destruction remains." The chestnut elixir awakens the sufferer from this darkness and shows him the way into the light that brings hope.

Rituals and Magical Use: Despite their longevity, chestnut trees lack the wealth of folklore that surrounds many other trees. Renown Bulgarian healer Petar Dimkov carried chestnuts with him and kept them under his pillow, due to their ability to radiate warmth and natural energy. To him, they were like guardian angels.

The nuts are also popular in talismans and amulets, because they attract wealth, success, prosperity, and happiness. If it's love you're looking for, chestnuts may be the solution, as they are ingredients in magical drinks and love potions. A remedy to cure a startled and frightened man was to add three dry chestnuts and sow-thistle to three glasses of old wine and have the man drink it early in the morning and late at night.

Chestnuts can also cleanse bad energy from your home, especially that created by quarreling and family conflicts. To achieve this, gather as many of the nuts as you can, but do it on a Monday. Once you return home, place the nuts in all the corners of every room. Don't touch them for three days while the nuts absorb all the negativity circulating through the house. Finally, on Thursday of that same week, you'll want to get rid of the nuts, but you mustn't touch them with your hands. Use a paper towel or cloth to gather them and deposit them into a bag. Take them outside and bury the nuts under leaves, but not too close to your house. Recite a little chant while you do this: "They cleaned my house, absorbed all the bad things. I return the fruits of the earth to the earth. I save myself and my home from evil."

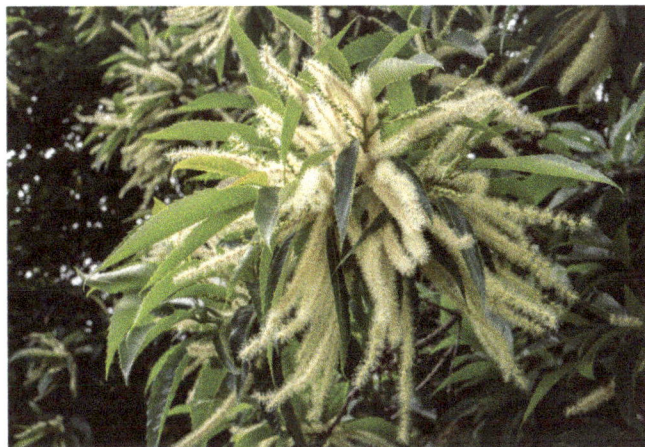

Other Use: Chestnut is popular in landscaping and as a shade tree, and its twigs are used in bouquets, floral arrangements, and other crafts. Its light-colored hardwood is also suitable for carving, furniture, barrels, roof beams, and fence posts. It's a good fuel source, but not for open fires since it spits sparks as it burns.

After the prickly shell is removed, the edible chestnuts can be eaten raw, baked, or roasted in their hard brown shells. They are popular as a stuffing ingredient. Chestnuts are used when brewing Corsican beer, and the French preserve the nuts in a fruits-of-the-earth syrup for a sweet delicacy. Powdered nuts are a flour substitute, and roasted seeds can be used as a coffee substitute.

The seed meal contains starch and can be used to whiten linen. Also, a decoction of leaves and fruit skins can even be used to make a shampoo to add a golden hue to hair.

Other Names: Sweet chestnut, chestnut, husked nut, Jupiter's nut, Spanish chestnut, European chestnut, common chestnut, Eurasian chestnut, Sardian nut.

Aromatic: The pollen has an unpleasant aroma. The raw nuts are bitter because of the high concentration of tannins, but baked, the nuts have a sweet taste and floury texture.

SOURCES

Abbott, George Frederick. *Macedonian Folklore*. Cambridge: University Press, 1903. https://hdl.handle.net/2027/uc1.$b98052.

Atanasov, Kostadin. "Spa vacation on Christmas and New Year's Eve." December 21, 2013. https://bnr.bg/en/post/100276927/spa-vacation-on-christmas-and-new-years-eve.

Dimitrova, M. "Магическите свойства на кестените: Личен талисман и пречистване на дома." [The Magic Properties of Chestnuts: Personal Mascot and Purification of the Home.] September 17, 2019. https://www.woman-onthe-top.net/p/magicheskite-svojstva-na-kestenite-lichen-talisman-i-prechistvane-na-doma/.

Fine Dining Lovers Editorial Staff. "How to Store Chestnuts at Home: 8 Easy Ways." October 22, 2018. https://www.finedininglovers.com/article/how-to-store-chestnuts-at-home.

Kosňovská, Jitka. "The origin, Archaeobotany and ethnobotany of Sweet Chestnut (*Castanea sativa* Miller) in the Czech Republic." *IANSA* IV, no. 2 (2013): 163-176. https://www.academia.edu/9540631/The_Origin_Archaeobotany_and_Ethnobotany_of_Sweet_Chestnut_Castanea_sativa_Miller_in_the_Czech_Republic.

Markov, Alexander. "Associate Professor Stefka Tepavicharova develops products fighting stress and aging." February 27, 2014. https://bnr.bg/en/post/100337191/associate-professor-stefka-tepavicharova-develops-products-fighting-stress-and-aging.

Missouri Botanical Garden. "Castanea sativa." https://www.missouribotanicalgarden.org/PlantFinder/PlantFinderDetails.aspx?taxonid=280759.

Online Etymology Dictionary. "Chestnut (n.)." https://www.etymonline.com/word/chestnut.

Petrova, Bilyana, Dr., ed. "Кестен-обикновен, Сладък кестен, Ядлив кестен." [Common chestnut, Sweet chestnut, Edible chestnut.] April 16, 2010, updated on September 14, 2021. https://medpedia.framar.bg/ботаника/кестен-обикновен-сладък-кестен-ядлив-кестен.

Picture This. "Sweet chestnut (Castanea sativa) Care Guide." https://www.picturethisai.com/care/Castanea_sativa.html.

Plants For A Future. "Castanea sativa - Mill." https://pfaf.org/user/plant.aspx?LatinName=Castanea+sativa.

Rxlist.com. "European Chestnut." June 11, 2021. https://www.rxlist.com/european_chestnut/supplements.htm.

WebMD Editorial Contributors. "Chestnuts: Health Benefits, Nutrition, and Uses." September 2, 2020. https://www.webmd.com/diet/health-benefits-chestnuts.

EUROPEAN CORNEL
Cornus mas

Cornus mas
European cornel

Cornel is a versatile wood and is part of both children's and adult activities. An interesting aspect of the plant's flower is that it will blossom at any time of the year when a branch or twig is set into water, even though cornel is not evergreen. Perhaps this is what makes the plant so magical, with the ability to bring health, happiness, and fertility throughout the year. The tree is also symbolic of longevity due to its tough and durable wood. This magical tree is believed to bring good health, a long life, and good luck. It's a plant that is an early bloomer, but also one that bears fruit later than most.

Description: Cornel grows to a height of 15 to 25 feet (5 to 8 meters). Its crown is rounded and spreads out 15 to 20 feet (5 to 6 meters). Young branches are thin and covered with hairs. They are green, turning brown as they age. Mature trunks are scaly with exfoliating bark.

Ovate to elliptical leaves with a pointed tip form in opposite pairs, a dark green on top and lighter on the bottom. The leaves have six to seven pairs of veins. In autumn, the leaves turn red.

Small yellow flowers grow on short stalks. Each blossom has four petals. Flowers appear before the leaves and form in clusters of ten to twenty-five. Although the flowers form early, in late winter or early spring, they don't produce fruit until mid-summer. This fruit is an elongated drupe that turns dark red when ripe. They are fleshy and contain one seed.

CAUTION: No known hazards, but always consult with a medical professional before using herbs medicinally. Pregnant and lactating women should avoid use due to lack of information on its safety.

Asia, and naturalized in other locations. It grows primarily in forests.

Growth: Deciduous shrub or tree. The flowers blossom around February to March, while the fruits mature between August and October. Cornel prefers full sun or partial shade, and can grow in most soils,

History and Traditions: The genus name comes from the Latin *cornu* for "horn." This may be due to the wood's strength and density. The specific name means "male" or "masculine" and was added to distinguish this plant from the wild, female version, the *Cornus sanguinea*. The common name comes from the fact the fruits resemble carnelian, a semi-precious gemstone.

In ancient Rome and Greece, the fruit was pickled when green and eaten like olives. The wood, however, has a history of use in war. The legendary Trojan horse was said to be made of this wood. It was also a wood used to make weapons, some with silver threads woven into it. World War II soldiers suffering from scurvy were treated with cornel that had been crushed and dried in a thin layer.

Habitat and Distribution: Cornel is native to central, eastern, and southern Europe and southwestern

---

God and the Devil Choose Trees

A story about the cornel tree says that when God came down from heaven, he arrived at a place where a single cornel stood alone. He sat beneath its branches. While he rested, he caught sight of his reflection in the water and commanded it to "Come out!" It did, but this shadow of God was the opposite to the Lord, because it was the Devil.

The two of them divided the plants between themselves. The Devil chose the cornel tree because it blossomed early, and he thought it would also produce fruit before many other trees. God, on the other hand, chose the cherry tree. While the cherry was bountiful with fruit, the cornel didn't produce any until autumn (Stavreva, 515).

including clay, although it prefers the soil to be moist, but well-drained. Normal lifespans are twenty to thirty years, although it's possible for them to live 100 years in good conditions. To avoid spread, remove sucker roots when they appear.

Harvesting: The fruits, bark, and wood are used. Pick the fruits in August to October when they are ripe and red. Soften and dry them in the shade in a cool, dry place to prevent mold growth, due to the plant's high percentage of moisture. Or dry them in a dehydrator at 158°F (70°C). Store them in bags in a dry place.

Medical Use: Cornel has antimicrobial and anti-inflammatory properties. Medical remedies are for lowering body temperatures, diarrhea, blood in urine, painful gums, anemia, fever, colds, urinary tract diseases, and liver and bile diseases. To treat diarrhea, boil 1 Tablespoon of cornel in 250 to 300 ml of water for 5 minutes. Drink three times a day before meals.

Rituals and Magical Use: One of children's best-loved traditions is the making of *survachki* on New Year's (Survaki). Another ritual using cornel takes place in March, the Feast of the Forty Martyrs, and also at each new moon. On this day, activities abound, involving the number forty. Girls go out at dawn and build small bridges made of forty cornel sticks and tie them with red thread. As the girls set the bridges over rivulets, they say, "May he who is my fate take me across this bridge tonight." In the evening, the girls put a piece of the first bite of bread under their pillow at night. If a boy leads them across their bridge in their dreams, he is destined to

---

Survachki, the Magical Wand

On New Year's, children gather a cornel branch or twig that's two to three feet long and tie the pairs of twigs that grow on each side of the stem together to make circles. Then they decorate their wand with an assortment of items: strings of popcorn, red thread, and small rings of bread are always popular, and unspun wool is often used among those who raise sheep.

The making of the *survachki* is only half the fun. Next, the children (usually boys between the ages of 4 and 12) visit relatives and neighbors to wish them health and prosperity throughout the year. They sing the blessing below while they tap the adults on the back with their "magic wand." In return, the children receive treats and coins from the adults.

Surva, surva year,
A merry year,
Golden wheat in the field,
Red apples in the orchard,
Plump grains of wheat in the field,
A house full of silk,
A large cluster of grapes on the vine,
Live healthy next year,
Till next year, Amen!

The tapping comes from ancient mystical rituals in which it was believed the branch's magic was transferred to those who held it, giving them prosperity, health, and long life (from *Light Love Rituals*).

become her fiancé. If no one appears in the dream, it means the bridge was destroyed.

The wedding flag (*uruglitza*) is made from cornel to symbolize health and fertility in a marriage. A special ritual is performed while cutting the pole for the flag. When the participants find a straight sapling, one of the party cuts off the branches with an axe and pours wine onto the roots. Bread and walnuts are left for any mythical being who might live there. The tree must be cut with a single stroke as close to the ground as possible. As they bring the tree back, the group sings songs.

Cornel has many other uses in Bulgarian beliefs.

- When the fruit ripens, it marks the time when the first *sedyanka* (half working-bee, half party where young people gather) is held, and when the yellow flowers appear in spring, then the last gathering is held.
- It is the wood of choice for instruments used during sacred rituals, such as the stick the first guest to enter the house on St. Ignatius Feast uses to poke the fire.
- On Budni vecher (Christmas Eve), the tree buds are placed on the table along with the food and are censed for health and luck.
- The buds are tossed into fires for divination. If they crack loudly like popcorn, it means health to the one who threw them.
- The number of fruits on a cornel provides a means of forecasting weather. When there are many, people believe the wheat harvest will be plentiful, but also winter will be long with much snow. A lot of fruits, in addition to numerous wild apples, indicates a cold winter with much snow.
- The buds may be swallowed for good health.
- Girls wash their hair in water the cornel branches soaked in to make their hair thick and long.
- To ensure health throughout the year, villagers passed through a hole formed from two trees tied together.

Other Use: Cornel is a showy plant and good for ornamental use or as a hedge. The hard wood was once compared to the strength of bones. The tree's wood is used to make handgun grips, tool handles, machine parts, and among the Bulgarians, *kavals* (shepherd's flutes) and the wooden parts of *gaidas* (bagpipes).

The fruit is edible and can be eaten raw, dried, or made into jam, jelly, juice, syrup, and preserves, along with wine, vodka, brandy, and liqueurs. Edible oil can be extracted from its seeds. Additionally, roasted seeds are ground into powder for a coffee substitute.

Other Names: Cornel, cornelian cherry dogwood, cornelian cherry, edible dogwood, sorbet.

Aromatic: Unripe fruit has a sweet-sour, astringent taste like cranberries and sour cherries, while ripened fruit is juicy, with a plum-like flavor.

SOURCES

Agapkina, Tatyanaa Alekseevna. "Деревья в славянской народной традиции: Очерки." [Trees in the Slavic folk tradition: Essays.] Indrik: Moscow, 2019. https://www.academia.edu/45107661/Деревья_в_славянской_народной_традиции_Очерки.

Ivanov, Ivan Isaev, Prof.; Iliya Ivanov Landzhev, Dr. of Pharmacy; Geo Kirilov Neshev, Dr. of Medicine. *Билките в България и използването им*. [Herbs in Bulgaria and their use.] Zemizdat: Sofia, 1977.

Konstantinova, Daniela. "Trees that Bulgarians venerate most." December 26, 2015. https://bnr.bg/en/post/100635118/trees-that-bulgarians-venerate-most.

MacDermott, Mercia. *Bulgarian Folk Customs*. London and Philadelphia: Jessica Kingsley Publishers, 1998.

Missouri Botanical Garden. "Cornus mas." https://www.missouribotanicalgarden.org/PlantFinder/PlantFinderDetails.aspx?kempercode=c290.

Nedelcheva, Anely and Yunus Dogan. "Usage of plants for weather and climate forecasting in Bulgarian folk traditions." *Indian Journal of Traditional Knowledge* 10, no. 1 (January 2011): 91-95. https://www.academia.edu/12909328/Usage_of_plants_for_weather_and_climate_forecasting_in_Bulgarian_folk_traditions.

Petrova, Bilyana, Dr., ed. "Дрян обикновен." [Common dogwood.] March 23, 2010, updated on January 24, 2020. https://medpedia.framar.bg/ботаника/дрян-обикновен.

Plants For A Future. "Cornus mas - L." https://pfaf.org/user/Plant.aspx?LatinName=Cornus+mas.

Stavreva, Lilia. *Български магии и гадания*. [Bulgarian magic and divination.] Trud Publishing House: Sofia, 2007.

HAZEL
Corylus avellana

Corylus avellana
Hazel

The hazel tree may not be the first tree you think of if someone asked you what is your favorite, but its nuts are among the healthiest. It also has some unique myths to make it special.

Description: Hazel normally grows to a height of around 6.5 to 13 feet (2 to 4 meters) or to tree size of 26 to 30 feet (8 to 9 meters), with a rounded crown spreading to 8 to 10 feet (2.5 to 3 meters). The bark is smooth and ash-colored or grayish-brown and covered with white, brown, or yellow spots. As it ages, it develops a crisscross pattern, and the bark may lightly flake in strips.

Leaves alternate and have an ovate shape with a heart-shaped base, sharp tip, and double-toothed, uneven edge. They are dark green on top and lighter underneath, with both sides having fine hairs. Leaves turn yellow in autumn.

Male and female flowers both grow on the same plant. Yellowish-brown to yellowish-gray males grow in catkins, while females are inconspicuous and bloom hidden within a green bud just above the catkins. Flowers bloom before the leaves develop. The fruit the females produce is the hazelnut, also called the cob nut. It's encased in a leafy, hairy, green husk. The nut has a spherical to oval shape with dark brown skin. They can grow alone or in groups of two to five on a single stalk.

History and Traditions: The genus name comes from the Greek *korylos* or *korys*, which means "helmet," referring to the nut's husk, and the specific name refers to a town in Italy: either Avella Veccia or Avellino.

Cno is the Celtic word for "nuts," and *cnocach* for "wisdom." The Celts tell a tale of how hazelnuts impart the knowledge of the world to any who eat them. Once, nine hazel trees grew on the border between the human and godly worlds, and these trees dropped their nuts into a stream. Salmon ate the nuts and became all-knowing, the Salmon of Wisdom. Not only did they become wise, but so did anyone who ate the salmon.

Celts considered the flexible hazel branches magical wands. According to tradition, the diviner will cut the wand with a new knife on St. John's Day.

In the early 1900s, the Contorta cultivar was given the common name of Harry Lauder's Walking Stick in honor of the Scottish entertainer (1870–1950), due to its twisted branches.

Habitat and Distribution: Native to Europe, western Asia, and northern Africa. The plant grows at the borders of woodlands, in hedgerows, on hill slopes, and along streams.

Growth: Deciduous tree. Hazel blossoms between January and April, and the fruits mature between late August and October. The tree bears fruit after its first four years or up to ten years, then yearly after that. The plant grows best in full sun to partial shade

---

CAUTION: The nuts are safe for most people in moderate dietary amounts. Use caution, however, if you have allergies to other tree nuts. There is a lack of information about their safety for pregnant or lactating women.

in moist, rich, well-drained soil, but it can tolerate other soils, but not heavy clay.

Harvesting: The nuts, leaves, bark, branches, wood, and twig bark are used. Nuts tend to mold quickly, so it's best to dry them in the shade, spread out in a thin layer. Store them at low temperatures and low humidity. Peel off the bark around April or May and dry in the shade or in a dehydrator at 122°F (50°C). When dry, the bark will be brownish-gray.

Medical Use: The nuts contain healthy nutrients and are good for those who suffer from anemia, type 2 diabetes, or insomnia. A study has also shown benefits of hazelnuts for cataracts (caused by chemotherapy drugs). They are also consumed to improve memory and the ability to sleep. Medicinal extracts from the leaves are traditionally used externally for relief of hemorrhoids, and leaves and bark both are treatments for varicose veins and other skin irritations, such as sunburn, diaper rash, eczema, and insect bites. Drinking tea from the leaves is good for sore throats or diarrhea.

Rituals and Magical Use: Special powers attributed to hazel include good luck, success, happiness, fertility, protection, and wishes. Anyone who sees hazel blossoming will always be happy. If you miss

---

Hermes's Caduceus

Hermes (or Mercury), the messenger of the Greek gods, is portrayed not only with his winged sandals but also with a caduceus. Originally, it was a rod or an olive branch entwined with ribbons and was a symbol of peace. Later on, two snakes encircled the staff, which was now winged. The staff was made from hazel wood and was magical. Anyone Hermes touched with the staff would fall asleep. It could also tell if a person died peacefully or terribly (Whalen).

Visitor's Blessings

On St. Barbara's Day (December 4) families prepared a special meal for the *polaznik*, an outside visitor who came to wish them a happy new year. He placed hazel twigs near the hearth and sat on them while he stirred embers in the hearth and gave blessings to the family. These would include the health of the family and the fertility of their animals. When the *polaznik* left, the wife of the family placed the twigs he had sat on in among the hens to encourage them to lay more eggs (MacDermott, 158-159).

out on this, you can sew fused nuts into your clothing to get the same effect. In some places, a child's godmother would sew hazel into the child's clothing, which he would wear until the age of three or four. If the piece of clothing was lost, the child would be unhappy all of his life.

Diviners use the twigs for dowsing rods, and the wood can be used as magical wands. These are most powerful if you stand facing the east while you cut the branch sometime after sunset but before sunrise.

You can also bless a room by sweeping a branch around the edges as you move clockwise around the room. Hazel crowns were once believed to bring invisibility as well as grant wishes. To have general luck, you can hang strings of nuts around your home. The nuts also grant fertility to a bride, as well as provide wisdom and divination to those who eat the nuts. Anyone who had trouble remembering things can be led three times around a hazel bush to restore his memory.

Another ability of hazel is for divination about one's fate or even to recognize a thief. You can use the nuts to reveal past or future secrets and give a person the ability to discover the truth. On Christmas Eve, it's a Bulgarian custom to crack a nut.

A light kernel foretells health for the coming year. If it's black, the person is certain to get sick.

To gain an understanding of the language of animals, a person must put into his mouth the meat of a snake that had lived under a hazel tree. Eating that same snake's heart grants the consumer the knowledge of medicinal herbs.

Hazel has power over snakes and their bites. On certain days of the year, snakes can be driven out of their lairs with a hazel twig. In addition, anyone who holds onto a branch on these days does so with the hope that a snake won't bite them during the year. And, if they get bitten, they can rub the injury with hazel leaves. Shepherds also make a staff from hazel to protect themselves and their cattle from snake bites.

While some trees attract lightning, people believed that hazel would deflect it. This is because devils run away from hazel. During a storm, the lightning is aiming directly for these devils. Therefore, if someone is caught outside during a thunderstorm, he can hide beneath the maple to keep safe. Carrying a piece of hazel on themselves or on their hat, particularly if the twig has hazel fruits, is also a way to ensure they won't be struck by lightning. Hazel holds this power because it has its own "fire," a piece of heavenly fire.

To protect the home from lightning, people place hazel twigs on their window frame or attach a hazel rod to the highest point of the roof and place another one behind a ceiling beam.

The Bulgarians have a proverb about the nuts: "If it thunders on St. Elijah's Day (July 20), walnuts and hazelnuts won't be born." Additionally, an abundant crop of hazelnuts is a weather forecast for a terrible winter. Winter will be even more severe if, besides many hazelnuts, crops of sloes (*Prunus spinosa*) and walnuts (*Juglans regia*) are also plentiful.

Hazel is important in other aspects of Bulgarian culture. The pole of the wedding banner can be made from hazel, since the wood must be light enough for the person who carries it to be able to dance the *horo*, a popular circle dance. The wood must also be easily broken, because the banner will be dismantled at the end of the wedding ceremony.

Additionally, in earlier times among Bulgarians, a piece of hazel was one means by which a corpse was measured, so the grave diggers and coffin-maker had accurate measurements. The piece of hazel was afterwards placed in the coffin and buried with the corpse.

Other Use: Hazel is a common plant for hedges, its wood is soft and makes a suitable material for wood carving, and artists use the charcoal for drawing. The oil from the plant makes a good wood polish. Hazel's branches have been used to weave beehives and baskets as well.

Hazelnuts can be eaten raw, roasted, or ground into a paste. The nut's oil is used in cooking and cosmetics. In particular, the seeds are finely ground to make face masks.

Other Names: Common hazel, hazelnut, European hazelnut, cobnut, hale nut, stock nut, wood nut.

Aromatic: The nuts are bitter.

SOURCES

Agapkina, Tatyana Alekseevna. "Деревья в славянской народной традиции: Очерки." [Trees in the Slavic folk tradition: Essays.] Indrik: Moscow, 2019. https://www.academia.edu/45107661/Деревья_в_ славянской_народной_традиции_Очерки.

Cunningham, Scott. *Cunningham's Encyclopedia of Magical Herbs*. Llewellyn: Woodbury, MN, 2012.

European trees. "Hazel, Filbert, *Corylus avellana*." http://www.european-trees.com/hazel.html.

Iliev, A.T. "Растевеята отъ българско фолклорно гледище." [Plants from the Bulgarian folklore point of view.] *Historical and Philological Journal*, May 18, 1916. http://parks.bg/wp-content/uploads/ 2016/07/11.-Iliev-At.-Rasteniyata_ot_bylgarskoto_folkorno_gledishte.pdf.

Ivanov, Ivan Isaev, Prof.; Iliya Ivanov Landzhev, Dr. of Pharmacy; Geo Kirilov Neshev, Dr. of Medicine. *Билките в България и използването им*. [Herbs in Bulgaria and their use.] Zemizdat: Sofia, 1977.

MacDermott, Mercia. *Bulgarian Folk Customs*. London and Philadelphia: Jessica Kingsley Publishers, 1998.

Missouri Botanical Garden. "Corylus avellana 'Contorta.' " https://www.missouribotanicalgarden.org/ PlantFinder/PlantFinderDetails.aspx?kempercode=c360.

Nedelcheva, Anely and Yunus Dogan. "Usage of plants for weather and climate forecasting in Bulgarian folk traditions." *Indian Journal of Traditional Knowledge* 10, no. 1 (January 2011): 91-95. https://www.academia.edu/12909328/Usage_of_plants_for_weather_and_climate_forecasting_in_ Bulgarian_folk_traditions.

Petrova, Bilyana, Dr. "Лешник, Леска, Обикновена леска, Обикновен лешник." [Hazelnut, Hazel, Common hazel, Common hazelnut.] April 7, 2010, updated on July 29, 2022. https://medpedia.framar.bg/ботаника/леска.

Plants For A Future. "Corylus avellana - L." https://pfaf.org/user/plant.aspx?LatinName=Corylus+avellana.

The Present Tree. "Every Hazel Tree Has a Story…" October 5, 2021. https://thepresenttree.com/blogs/tree-meanings/hazel-tree-meaning.

Whalen, Ed. "The Caduceus: Magical Staff of Hermes." December 11, 2020. https://classicalwisdom.com/culture/the-caduceus-magical-staff-of-hermes/.

Whitehurst, Tess. *The Magic of Trees*. Llewellyn: Woodbury, MN, 2021.

HAWTHORN

Crataegus monogyna

Crataegus monoguna
Hawthorn

Hawthorn is connected to both the sacred and the impure. It symbolizes the Virgin Mary, whose life was filled with troubles. Additionally, some people associate the crown of thorns placed on Jesus's head with hawthorn, although others say the thorns came from the *Euphorbia milii*, while Christian scholars claim it was the *Ziziphus spina-christi*. But hawthorn also has many magical properties that enable it to protect people from evil.

Description: This prickly plant grows to a height of 15 to 20 feet (5 to 6 meters) with a dense crown that spreads about 20 feet (6 meters). The dull-brown bark has deep vertical fissures, revealing grayish-brown upper layers and orange lower ones. The shiny branches have a brownish-purple color, with the stiff reddish-brown or greenish twigs having brown buds and a small number of hairs. Some twigs sport thorns.

Shiny oval leaves are dark green on top and a lighter green underneath, with a pink-tinged stem. They are

CAUTION: Children and pregnant and lactating women should avoid hawthorn medically since its safety has not been studied. Those with heart disease and taking medications should consult a physician before using. The fruit's seeds contain cyanide bonded with sugar, which changes to hydrogen cyanide in the small intestine, and can be deadly if more than one or two seeds are eaten.

lobed into three to seven segments, and they're pointed and prickly. They turn scarlet-red in autumn.

Flowers cluster in groups of five to twenty-five, each having five petals. They are white or creamy and tinged pink. They bear many dark-red oval haws in groups of up to five that contain one seed.

History and Traditions: The genus name comes from the Greek *Krataigos*. This is the ancient name for a flowering thorn, with *kratos* meaning "strength" for its tough wood and *akis*, "sharp tip," because of its thorns. The specific name means "one seed." The common name of hawthorn comes from the Anglo-Saxon *haguthorn* for "a fence with thorns."

Hawthorn use can be traced as far back as the Roman Empire, being an important part of spring celebrations and weddings. The tree once played a role in May Day festivities and was called the May-Tree, named after the Greek goddess Maia. People decorated the maypole with hawthorn as they celebrated spring's renewal and fertility. Sprigs of hawthorn were part of ancient Greek weddings to bring the new couple happiness and prosperity.

In a medieval recipe from around 1390, the plant was an ingredient in *spinee*, an almond milk-based pottage. The flowers and berries have also been used for medicine, and the thorns made into fish hooks, sewing awls, and lances to pierce both blisters and ears.

It's been said that in 63 A.D., Joseph of Arimathea brought the first hawthorn to England and planted his staff, where it turned into a holy thorn, which bloomed each Christmas.

Habitat and Distribution: Native to Europe, northwestern Africa, and western Asia, and naturalized in North America, Australia, and other parts of the world. The plant grows in woodlands, hedgerows, thickets, and other scrub areas.

Dealing with Slavic Vampires

The Slavic vampire has some characteristics that are familiar to the western vampire: He is "undead," sleeps in his grave or coffin during the day, and drinks blood at night. However, among the Bulgarians and other Slavs, some types of vampires have no bones. Instead, they are shapeless, jelly-like bags of blood. As one drinks more blood, the vampire begins to regain a human form. Forty days after his burial, he'll look no different from any other human, although he still lacks bones. This absence of a solid structure makes him susceptible to anything that will cut or prick him. And so, one way to destroy him is to prick him with a hawthorn thorn. One touch and he'll burst, leaving only a pool of blood and a jelly-like substance.

It's best not to wait until the vampire gets to this human-like stage. If you suspect a person has become a vampire (and there are many ways that can happen, too many to write about here), you have options to keep him in his grave. Vampires never walk around on a Saturday, so you can dig up the grave and place hawthorn inside. A preferable (and more legal method) is to surround the grave with hawthorn.

You can stab the vampire with a hawthorn stake or pierce his heel with a thorn. If a deceased person was even suspected of returning as a vampire, a single thorn was put into his bellybutton to keep him in his grave. Problem solved. If he's out and about troubling your home, however, you'll have to resort to surrounding the outside of your entire home with a protective circle of hawthorn branches (MacDermott, 66-68; V, Stefan).

is of an age ready to produce fruit, but hawthorn can also grow in semi-shade.

Harvesting: The flowers, leaves, roots, and fruits are used. Harvest leaves and flowers between April and June. Prune small branches when the flowers begin to open, but have not yet reached full bloom. They have a fishy smell, but it will disappear after the flowers have dried. You can dry them in the shade in baskets, paper bags, or by hanging them in bundles. Or, you can dry them in a dehydrator at 104°F (40°C). In late summer or autumn, collect the berries when they are ripe and dry them in baskets or a dehydrator at the same temperature as the flowers.

Medical Use: Hawthorn is a remedy for heart problems, having a calming effect that dilates blood vessels, thereby improving blood supply to the heart and brain. The Bulgarian prophetess Baba Vanga claimed drinking a decoction made from hawthorn flowers four times a year was a way to prevent heart disease.

Likewise, hawthorn lowers blood pressure, calms the nervous system, and improves sleep. The herb was one of my grandmother's favorite cures. She added a few drops of hawthorn along with some of valerian onto a sugar cube whenever she felt stressed or had to endure major challenges in her life. Considering she lived to 99, she was able to successfully overcome these problems with her herbal cures.

Other folk medicine uses are for shortness of breath, enlarged prostate, and urinary problems.

Rituals and Magical Use: Among the most powerful use of hawthorn is its ability to protect against evil beings, who can be stopped from entering or exiting a place with the plant's thorns. They are particularly effective against vampires, who would immediately die when coming in contact with the plant. If the deceased had not yet risen as a vampire, but was suspected of doing so, placing a thorn on him inside his casket would keep him in the grave.

Growth: Deciduous shrub or tree. The plant blooms between April and June and bears fruits from September to November. In about five to eight years, seedling trees begin to bear fruit, while grafted trees may blossom after three years. The hawthorn is a medium growth plant and reaches its full height in about twenty to fifty years.

The plant is hardy and can grow in most soils (sandy, loamy, and clay), with the exception of wet peat or acidic sands, although it prefers moist, well-drained, loamy soil. Hawthorn can tolerate strong winds, drought, and pollution. Full sun is best when the plant

Witches can also try to get into your home. They love to fly down through the chimney. So while you're placing hawthorn around your home, put some in the chimney as well. During the Dirty Days (the time between Ignatius Feast on December 20 and the Epiphany on January 6), you'll want to put it around the doors and windows, too, as this is a time when evil beings are active. If you simply want to walk around outside in peace, carry a hawthorn stick or wand with you. It's certain to chase away any evil creature and allow you to travel safely at night.

On a completely different note, hawthorn is used to bring fertility. In Bulgaria, it's popular on St. George's Day, April 23. People decorate their homes with it and it's used in rites celebrated on that day. Shepherds also use hawthorn to decorate the vessels they collect milk with.

Hawthorn is another plant that is used for weather forecasting in Bulgarian folk belief. If hawthorn along with wild apples are plentiful, get ready to endure a bad winter.

Other Use: Hawthorn is commonly planted as a hedge. Its wood is a good fuel source as it produces much heat, but little smoke. The wood is hard and tough and is suitable for making tool handles, boxes, and boat parts. Hawthorn's fine grain also makes it a good wood for furniture.

The flowers, fruits, leaves, and shoots are edible, but don't eat the fruit's seeds (see caution box). Fruits are high in pectin, so they are added to other fruit to make jams and preserves, and the flowers are used in syrups and sweet puddings. The fruits are also used to make wines and ketchup. They can also be dried, ground, and combined with flour. Roasted seeds are a coffee substitute.

Young leaves, once known as "bread and cheese," can be added to salads or dried for tea. Flowers and buds can be as well, but discard any that smell like almonds when crushed. Hawthorn is a honey plant, with bees producing a dark amber, nutty honey from the flowers.

Other Names: Common hawthorn, one-seed hawthorn, one-seeded hawthorn, single-seeded hawthorn, European hawthorn, May tree, May-tree, whitethorn.

Aromatic: When the flowers first open, they have a scent with balsamic undertones. Later on, they have an unpleasant odor like decaying fish to attract insects for fertilization. The raw young shoots have a nutty flavor. The fruits are pulpy with a delicate taste.

SOURCES

Deane. "Hawthorn Harvest." https://www.eattheweeds.com/the-crataegus-clan-food-poison-2/.

Eat Weeds. "Hawthorn." https://www.eatweeds.co.uk/hawthorn-crataegus-monogyna.

eFloras.org. "Flora of North America." http://www.efloras.org/florataxon.aspx?flora_id=1&taxon_id=108272.

Harash, Rinat. "Christ's 'crown of thorns' tree may help in climate change fight: researchers." March 29, 2018. https://www.reuters.com/article/us-religion-easter-tree/christs-crown-of-thorns-tree-may-help-in-climate-change-fight-researchers-idUSKBN1H50VS.

Ivanov, Ivan Isaev, Prof.; Iliya Ivanov Landzhev, Dr. of Pharmacy; Geo Kirilov Neshev, Dr. of Medicine. *Билките в България и използването им.* [Herbs in Bulgaria and their use.] Zemizdat: Sofia, 1977.

Krohn, Elise. "Hawthorn." http://wildfoodsandmedicines.com/hawthorn/.

MacDermott, Mercia. *Bulgarian Folk Customs.* London and Philadelphia: Jessica Kingsley Publishers, 1998.

Medicinal Herbal Plants. "Baba Vanga – SPA." http://medicinal-herbal.blogspot.com/2012/01/baba-vanga-spa.html.

Nedelcheva, Anely and Yunus Dogan. "Usage of plants for weather and climate forecasting in Bulgarian folk traditions." *Indian Journal of Traditional Knowledge* 10, no. 1 (January 2011): 91-95. https://www.academia.edu/12909328/Usage_of_plants_for_weather_and_climate_forecasting_in_Bulgarian_folk_traditions.

Petrova, Bilyana, Dr., ed. "Глог, Червен глог, Бял глог, Глогинка." [Hawthorn, Red Hawthorn, White Hawthorn, Hawthorn.] March 22, 2010, updated on December 9, 2021. https://medpedia.framar.bg/ботаника/глог-червен-глог-бял-глог-глогинка.

Plants For A Future. "Crataegus monogyna – Jacq." https://pfaf.org/user/Plant.aspx?LatinName=Crataegus+monogyna.

Stavreva, Lilia. *Български магии и гадания.* [Bulgarian magic and divination.] Trud Publishing House: Sofia, 2007.

V., Stefan. "The Cult Of The Trees in Slavic Mythology." https://www.slavorum.org/the-cult-of-the-trees-in-slavic-mythology/.

QUINCE
Cydonia oblonga

Cydonia oblonga
Quince

Quince is a rather literary fruit. Perhaps it's the name that attracts writers to include it in stories. Normally, it's mentioned as a single tree in among others in a garden, a tree characters congregated beneath. The reference people recall the most, however, is likely the rhyme from Edward Lear's poem, "The owl and the pussy cat," which says, "They dined on mince, and slices of quince, / Which they ate with a runcible spoon."

Description: Quince grows to a height of 10 to 26 feet (3 to 8 meters), with a rounded, dense crown spreading 13 to 26 feet (4 to 8 meters). The plant is multi-stemmed and has blackish-brown crooked branches. Gray, grayish-brown, or grayish-black flaky bark covers the trunk, and young branches have velvety hairs.

Ovate to elliptical leaves alternate along the twig. They are darker green on top and paler, almost white, on the underside, which is covered with thick white hairs. The leaves turn yellow in autumn.

Large five-petaled flowers are pale-pink or white, and they grow from the leaf axils. The flowers produce a pear- or apple-shaped fruit, which is initially green and covered with grayish-white hairs. The fruit turns bright yellow when it ripens, and most of the hairs have rubbed off. Quince has eight to ten brown seeds.

History and Traditions: The genus name is derived from the ancient city state of Kydonai (now called

CAUTION: The seeds produce hydrogen cyanide in the stomach. If large quantities are consumed, they are toxic and can lead to respiratory failure and death. Pregnant and lactating women should avoid its use.

Chania) in northwest Crete. It's likely the Greeks imported grafts of the tree from Crete, which had a superior strain. The specific name is Latin for "oblong," referring to the shape of the fruits or leaves. "Quince" comes from the mid-fourteenth century English *quoyn*, or *coin*, which is derived from the Latin *cotoneum malum* for "quince apple."

Quince belongs to a group of plants that evolved around fifty million years ago and was cultivated around the Mediterranean during the Archaic period. Throughout the ages, it's been used to alleviate constipation, and lotions and compresses from the quince juice were used to relieve hemorrhoidal pain. Additionally, it was a treatment for periodontal disease, and Hippocrates suggested it be used as a tonic for the gastrointestinal tract.

Ancient Greeks consumed the fruits, candied in honey, at feasts. In Greek mythology, quince was sacred to Aphrodite and was a ritual offering at weddings. In order to sweeten their breath, brides nibbled quince before they entered the bridal chamber. Quince was called "a golden apple" and may have been the true fruit (rather than an apple) that Paris gave to Aphrodite in the beauty contest.

In Greek mythology, Acontius used a quince to trick his beloved Cydippe into marrying him. He plucked a fruit from Aphrodite's orchard, wrote on the skin, and rolled the fruit into the garden. His beloved read aloud the words "I swear by Aphrodite that I will marry Acacias," a vow that couldn't be broken. In some versions of the story, each time she was betrothed to another, she became ill. Finally, after consulting the Delphic oracle, they discovered that she must marry Acacias.

In the Balkans, a quince tree is planted when a baby is born. It symbolizes fertility, love, and life. On the other hand, the fruit is also one that may have been the "forbidden fruit" from the Garden of Eden.

Habitat and Distribution: Native to western and centra Asia. The plant grows on rocky slopes and at the edges of forests.

Growth: Deciduous tree or shrub. The plant blossoms between April and June, and the fruit ripens around October or November. For the best growth and flowering, it prefers full sun, although it can also grow in partial shade. The plant can tolerate deep shade, but most likely will not produce fruit. The best soil is well-drained loam, but quince trees can also adapt to other soil conditions. Once the plant is established, it can tolerate drier soil.

Harvesting. Fruits and seeds are used. It's best to harvest the fruit before the first frost. Fruit can be dried whole or thinly sliced. Wash them well before cutting and afterward, completely remove the seeds. Add 1 teaspoon of salt per liter of water and dip the

---

Cough Remedy

I use quince in a remedy for bad coughs. Combine two to three whole cracked walnuts, one quince chopped with the seeds, and a few onion skins. Boil for about 15 minutes in 1 liter of water. After it cools, drink it sweetened with honey and also a little cinnamon.

Quince and Apple Marmalade

Add 2 quarts of water into a pot. Quickly pare and slice 4 lbs. each of apples and quinces. Cook the quinces over low heat until they turn soft. Don't let them turn red from cooking too long. Strain them. Boil the sliced apples along with the quince juice for 45 minutes. Take it off the heat when it begins to boil and add 1.5 lbs. of sugar. When the sugar dissolves, return it to the burner and add the strained quinces. Cook for 20 minutes, constantly stirring and removing the scum. Add the resulting marmalade into a jar (Botanical.com).

Leaves have been used to treat nervousness, insomnia, and other problems, and bark for ulcers. Quince has also been used in treating cancer, diabetes, hepatitis, urinary infections, liver diseases, and more.

Rituals and Magical Use: Quince has powers of protection, love, and happiness. Carrying a seed will protect you from evil, physical harm, and accidents. The fruit was used during worship to the goddess of love. Newly married couples in Roman times ate quince together so that their future would be happy. Quince is given as a sign of love, and it's believed that if you serve quince to a loved one, he or she will remain faithful. In Bulgaria, young women prepared for their wedding by sewing under the shadow of the quince.

A ritual using quince leaves is performed to ensure love and to protect against loneliness. For this, a person picks two quince leaves. Then, barefoot, she goes outside and looks at the moon through a gap in the two leaves. She waves a white cloth toward the moon with her left hand, wraps the leaves in it, and then places the cloth beneath the pillow. During the night, the loved one appears in her dreams. The next day, she wraps one of the leaves in the cloth and buries it beneath a fruit tree. She dries and crumbles the other leaf along with a few vervain (*Verbena officinalis*) leaves. Finally, she carries it in her pocket until she meets her loved one. Then, in order to keep the love alive, she sprinkles the crushed leaves around the same fruit tree where she buried the other leaf.

The quince tree also thought highly of itself in songs, where it praises itself by saying, "There is nothing better than me in the garden."

Other Use: Quince is a popular rootstock for pears and other fruit trees. Because of the plant's large, showy flowers, the shrub form of the quince is grown as a hedge or ornamental border. Wood from the tree is used in making furniture and cabinets,

pieces in for about 3 minutes. Place the slices on a wire rack and dry them in the shade. Take them in at night and return them outside at sunrise until the fruits dry. Store them in tightly closed plastic bags in a dry room, out of direct sunlight. Nutritional value is best preserved by drying the fruit in a deyhdrator. Store fresh fruit in cool, well-ventilated rooms. Seeds used for medicinal purposes should be dried at 104°F (40°C) and no higher than 122°F (50°C).

Medical Use: Quince has many medicinal uses. The fresh fruit is used for anemia, while fiber in the fruit helps with digestion and fighting against obesity. To improve your mood, you can drink quince juice.

For diarrhea, ingest a syrup made from the unripe fruit. Juice from the quince also helps treat mouth ulcers, gum problems, and sore throats. Additionally, quince juice, combined with lemon juice, helps treat asthma. The juice and pulp, when used regularly, aid in healing stomach issues and eliminate vomiting.

When the seeds are soaked in water, they produce a mucilage, which can be taken internally to treat respiratory diseases, particularly in children, and help heal dermal wounds. In addition, a lotion made from the mucilage helps with eye and ear diseases. It can also be applied to burns and other skin injuries.

and mucilage from the seeds can add luster to various materials. To soften skin, you can make a decoction from the fruit, and to help get rid of gray hair, use a solution made from the leaves. Additionally, an enzyme in the plant acts as a way to treat industrial wastewater.

The fruit is mostly cooked to make it soft and juicy, rather than eaten raw, since it is quite hard and sour. In more tropical climates, the fruit will become soft enough to eat raw. It's made into jams, jellies, candies, puddings, sweets, and brandy.

Other Names: Common quince. Synonyms: *Cydonia vulgaris*, *Pyrus cydonia*.

Aromatic: Although the uncooked fruit is sour, the cooked quince has a sweet, candy-like aroma, with a gritty flesh. When cooked, small amounts of it enhance the flavor of apple pies, applesauce, and jams. The mucilage from the chewed seeds smells and tastes like bitter almonds. The stem bark is astringent.

SOURCES

Biklolechenie.bg. "Дюля: полезни свойства и използването й при различни заболявания." [Quince: useful properties and its use in various diseases.] https://bilkolechenie.bg/article/dyulya-polezni-svoystva-i-izpolzvaneto-y-pri-razlichni-zabolyavaniya.

Bilki.bg. "Дюля, действие и приложение на билката." [Quince, action and application of the herb.] https://bilki.bg/dyulya.html.

Botanical.com. "Quince." https://botanical.com/botanical/mgmh/q/quince04.html.

Cunningham, Scott. *Cunningham's Encyclopedia of Magical Herbs*. Llewellyn: Woodbury, MN, 2012.

DBpedia. "About: Acontius." https://dbpedia.org/page/Acontius.

Harris, Stephen. "Plant 198, Cydonia oblonga Mill. (Rosaceae), Quince." https://herbaria.plants.ox.ac.uk/bol/plants400/Profiles/CD/Cydonia.

Iliev, A.T. "Растевеята отъ българско фолклорно гледище." [Plants from the Bulgarian folklore point of view.] Historical and Philological Journal, May 18, 1916. http://parks.bg/wp-content/uploads/2016/07/11.-Iliev-At.-Rasteniyata_ot_bylgarskoto_folkorno_gledishte.pdf.

Ivanov, Ivan Isaev, Prof.; Iliya Ivanov Landzhev, Dr. of Pharmacy; Geo Kirilov Neshev, Dr. of Medicine. *Билките в България и използването им*. [Herbs in Bulgaria and their use.] Zemizdat: Sofia, 1977.

Missouri Botanical Garden. "Cydonia oblonga." http://www.missouribotanicalgarden.org/PlantFinder/PlantFinderDetails.aspx?taxonid=286497.

Nursery Management. "Cydonia oblonga." May 2016. https://www.nurserymag.com/article/cydonia-oblonga/.

Online Etymology Dictionary. "Quince (n.)" Updated on March 6, 2021. https://www.etymonline.com/word/quince#etymonline_v_3204.

Petel.bg. "Магически ритуали за всякакви случаи." [Magic rituals for all occasions.] November 17, 2022. https://petel.bg/m/237758.

Petrova, Bilyana, Dr. "Дюля." [Quince.] March 23, 2010, updated on June 8, 2022. https://medpedia.framar.bg/ботаника/дюля.

Plants For A Future. "Cydonia oblonga – Miller." https://pfaf.org/user/plant.aspx?latinname=Cydonia+oblonga.

Stoyanoff, Rossi. "Как да изсушим дюли?" [How to dry quinces?] https://gotvach.bg/tips/a-746-Как_да_изсушим_дюли.

EUROPEAN BEECH
Fagus sylvatica

Fagus sylvatica
European beech

Oak may be the king of the forest, but beech is its queen or mother. The tree has a generous spirit, providing both shelter and nourishment. It's also a tree of wisdom, learning, knowledge, and understanding.

Description: Beech typically grows to a height of 100 to 130 feet (30 to 40 meters), although some may reach as high as 160 feet (50 meters). The dense crown has an oval to round shape, with a spread of 50 to 70 feet (15 to 21 meters). The tree's bark is gray and smooth, while one- to two-year-old branches are light brown and covered with hairs that eventually fall off. Branches droop and sweep the ground, and their wood is brittle.

Oval-shaped leaves alternate along the twig and have up to six or seven pairs of veins. The leaf edges are wavy and toothed. Young leaves have hairs along the edge and veins. The upper side of the leaves is shiny and dark green, while the underside is light green. In autumn, the leaves turn copper or golden-bronze and may remain on the tree during winter.

Both male and female yellowish-green flowers grow on the same plant. They are small and covered with hairs. Males form drooping clusters on long stems, while females grow on short spikes. The flowers produce spiny husks called cupules. When ripe, these cupules split into four segments to reveal beechnuts or masts, brown oval fruits with three pointed sides. Inside this shell lies a white seed.

CAUTION: Beech nuts may be toxic if consumed uncooked in large quantities, or if less severe, cause gastric problems. The toxins, however, will be broken down and made safe when heating or roasting the nuts for 3 to 5 minutes.

History and Traditions: The Latin genus name comes from the Greek *phegos*, which not only meant "beech," but also "edible" and sometimes "oak." The specific name is derived from the Latin *sylva* for "forest" and refers to something that grows in the woods or is forest-loving. The common name, besides describing the tree, can mean "book," denoting the fact early books were written on thin pieces of beech bark.

These books were believed to hold the magic and power of the gods. And the Celtic warrior god Ogma was said to have written the Ogham runic alphabet on beech. Although beech itself is not one of the runes for the months of the birth tree calendar, it is an additional consonant called *Phagos*. Among the Celts, forked branches of the beech tree were used for prophesying.

In more modern history, Gutenberg may have developed his inspiration for printing after he carved letters onto a beech tree. Then, after he wrapped the damp bark in paper, the letters were imprinted on the sheet.

Beech also has been used medically in the past. Poultices made from the leaves were applied to the skin to relieve swelling and boils. And it was taken internally as an expectorant for chronic bronchitis. During WWI, troops also tried unsuccessfully to use beech as a substitute for tobacco. Beech was also once thought to be deadly to snakes.

Habitat and Distribution: Native to central and southern Europe. In the mid-1700s, Europeans brought the tree to America. The trees grow in woodlands. Beech trees in southern England may have been brought there 12,000 years ago, after the last ice age receded.

Cough Remedy
Roast and grind 7 ounces (200 g) of the nuts. Mix them with 18 ounces (half a kilogram) of honey. Take 1 Tablespoon three to four times daily before meals (Petrova).

Fever Remedy
Saturate 2 Tablespoons of beech bark in 8 to 10 ounces (250 to 300 ml) of water and boil for a few minutes. Let the liquid cool, then strain it. Take 1 spoonful each hour throughout the day (Petrova).

Growth: Deciduous tree. The plant blossoms around April to May and its fruit ripens during September or October. Beech prefers full sun to partial shade, but can also grow in a full shade woodland area. The best soil will be rich and moist, but well-drained. A beech can tolerate drought, but its shallow root system makes it less resistant to strong winds and heavy snowfall. The trees can live up to 500 years.

Harvesting: All parts of the tree can be used medically. To harvest beechnuts, wait until the fruit turns brown and falls from the tree. Remove the outer spiky husk. Then, spread out the triangular nuts so they don't overlap. Allow the nuts to dry for two to three weeks in a well-ventilated area. Once the nuts dry, you can store them in their shell inside a jar for years. When you want to use them, it's easy to remove the outer shell with your fingernail to extract its seed.

Medical Use: Beech bark has antacid, antiseptic, and expectorant properties, among others. It helps reduce itching from eczema, psoriasis, and scabies, and the plant's pure creosote is a pain reliever for toothaches and bronchial inflammations. Other uses of beech are for lung inflammation, eye diseases, digestive issues, muscle and bone problems, and kidney disease. Charcoal from burned beech wood is used to make the medical charcoal use for intestinal gas, food poisoning, and other body intoxications.

Beech is one of the Bach's Thirty-eight Flowers. It's meant for those who are critical of how others act, speak, or do things, or those who lack compassion or are irritable. By using the elixir, a person will become more sensitive to the feelings of others and gain understanding and tolerance for the differences between people.

In Bulgarian folk medicine, European beech leaves are treatments for jaundice, fever, and spasms. Crushed leaves help reduce swellings on the skin and treat burns and frostbite, and you can chew the leaves for gum problems. A decoction made from beech twig or bark added to bath water helps with rheumatism. Beech ash is also used to tone skin or remove warts.

Rituals and Magical Use: Fairies or nymphs called Vily are partial to beech trees. The females give birth within the tree's branches, and they wrap their infants with the green leaves. In Bosnia, there's a beech forest called Vilina Shuma (Vila Forest), in which the branches of hundreds of trees are severely curved.

About the tree people say, "There is a lot of flour near the beech," which symbolizes stamina, strength, and greatness. It also represents firmness and is a means of punishment, such as a staff or club. In this respect, people say, "Because of the beeches, the forest is not visible."

To ancient Slavic tribes living in the mountains, beech was a totem-tree. It was called "the brother of the oak." And like the oak, it was used for a *budnik* log by some, but it could be cut only with permission. It was forbidden for young trees to be cut, however.

Beech is a tree of wishes. The thin beech bark is delicate and unable to heal itself when someone carves into it. Therefore, you can use it to make wishes. After carving your desire onto a stick, say a simple spell as you bury it. Your message on the wood will manifest if it is meant to be. Even Helen of Troy carved the name of her lover upon the tree.

Although beech cannot heal itself, if you spend time relaxing alone beneath its branches, the tree can help you heal deep emotional pain. Write down all your pains and be open to receiving healing guidance from the beech.

To increase creative powers or bring yourself luck, you can carry beech leaves or small pieces of the bark in your pocket or elsewhere on your person.

Other Use: Beech has many uses. The wood is hard and durable and bends without breaking, which makes it suitable for indoor use, such as for furniture, flooring, cooking utensils, and tool handles, among other things, such as drums. The leaf buds dried on the twigs can be used as toothpicks, and the dried leaves can be used as mattress filling. Beech seed oil is suitable for wood polish and is an ingredient in a variety of ointments. The oil can also be used in the making of soap. Suitable for fuel, the wood burns for many hours.

The nuts are used mostly for pig food, rather than for human consumption, but the seeds can be ground into powder and added to flour or roasted as a coffee substitute. Raw young leaves can be a salad ingredient or soaked in gin to create a liqueur.

After it has been processed to remove its flavor and aroma, beech wood has also been used in Budweiser beer fermentation tanks. The yeast settles on the wood surface without piling up and therefore prevents off-flavors in the beer. In some German smoked beers, beech logs are burned to dry the malt, and beech is also used to smoke hams, sausages, and cheeses.

Other Names: Beech, common beech.

Aromatic: The raw young leaves of European beech have a mild flavor, sweet but softer than a mild cabbage. The nuts are bitter when raw, but the flavor improves after roasting.

SOURCES

Adamant, Ashley, "Foraging Beech Nuts." September 28, 2018. https://practicalselfreliance.com/foraging-beech-nuts/.

Agapkina, Tatyana Alekseevna. "Деревья в славянской народной традиции: Очерки." [Trees in the Slavic folk tradition: Essays.] Indrik: Moscow, 2019. https://www.academia.edu/45107661/Деревья_в_славянской_народной_традиции_Очерки.

Aleksstosich. "Стабло живота – The Tree of Life." September 27, 2018. https://svilenkonac.net/2018/09/27/стабло-живота-the-tree-of-life/.

Alina. "Beechnuts: expert knowledge about the fruit of the beech tree." https://plantura.garden/uk/trees-shrubs/beech/beechnuts.

Anatolyevich, Kononenko Alexey. "Бук." [Beech.] https://history.wikireading.ru/406185.

Botanical.com. "Beech." https://botanical.com/botanical/mgmh/b/beech-27.html.

Cunningham, Scott. *Cunningham's Encyclopedia of Magical Herbs*. Llewellyn: Woodbury, MN, 2012.

Isabella. "The Magickal Beech Tree." July 11, 2017. https://speakingofwitchwands.net/2017/11/07/2357/.

Missouri Botanical Garden. "Fagus sylvatica." https://www.missouribotanicalgarden.org/PlantFinder/PlantFinderDetails.aspx?kempercode=a866.

Order of Bards, Ovates and Druids. "Beech." https://druidry.org/druid-way/teaching-and-practice/druid-tree-lore/beech.

Osborne, Jane. "The Mystic Magic of The Beech Tree – fagus sylvatica." July 12, 2018. https://jane-osborne.com/the-mystic-magic-of-the-beech-tree-fagus-sylvatica/.

Petrova, Bilyana, Dr. "Бук обикновен." [Common beech.] April 9, 2010, updated on November 30, 2022. https://medpedia.framar.bg/ботаника/бук-обикновен.

Plants For A Future. "Fagus sylvatica - L." https://pfaf.org/user/plant.aspx?LatinName=Fagus+sylvatica.

Trees of Stanford. "Fagus sylvatica." https://trees.stanford.edu/ENCYC/FAGsyl.htm.

Whitehurst, Tess. *The Magic of Trees*. Llewellyn: Woodbury, MN, 2021.

EUROPEAN ASH

Fraxinus excelsior

Fraxinus excelsior
European ash

into greenish-white or purplish dense clusters. The flowers on one tree may be male or female. Both sexes can also be on the same tree. Ash can even change its gender from year to year. The fruit it produces is a winged ash-key or samara, with the seed inside. They turn from green to brown as the seeds ripen. Fruits can form in groups of up to 150. They remain attached to the tree until the next spring, when the wind blows them off.

History and Traditions: The genus name is the Latin word for the tree. It comes from the Greek *phraxis* for "hedge" or the Latin *fraxinus* for "lightning," because ash is among those trees that, when isolated, attract lightning. The specific name is from the Latin *excelsus* for "lofty" or "high."

Ash is among those trees that are called a World Tree, Yggdrasil in Norse mythology, although scholars today claim that it was actually a yew tree.

A Neolithic tool from around 5000 B.C. was discovered with an ash handle. In more recent antiquity, ash trees were planted near castles, and their hard, flexible wood was used to make lances and bows. In Ovid's *Metamorphoses*, ash was called a "tree with spears."

Ash has a long history of medical use. It was once used as a treatment for snake bites. The belief was that the leaves were so powerful that snakes wouldn't dare touch the shadow of the tree in the morning or evening, or even crawl over its wood. Instead, they would make a large circle around the tree. Pliny the Elder conducted an experiment to see just how much snakes hated ash trees. Once when a snake was surrounded by ash leaves, Pliny lit a fire in the center of the circle. The snake was said to have crawled into the fire, rather than over the pile of leaves.

Ash is ranked among the noble hardwoods. This tree has both ethnic and mythological importance to many cultures. Even in our age, the tree has been on center stage, as it was the tree of the year in 2001 in Bulgaria.

Description: The ash tree grows to a height of around 70 to 80 feet (21 to 24 meters) or a maximum of around 130 to 150 feet (40 to 46 meters). Its rounded or irregular crown has a spread of 50 to 60 feet (15 to 18 meters). The light gray bark is smooth when the tree is young and becomes rough and scaly with a network of cracks after around thirty years.

Compound leaves are elliptical or lance-shaped and have four to eight pairs of leaflets, with a single leaf on top. Their edges are sharply toothed. The dark-green leaves are paler underneath, with somewhat hairy veins. The leaves turn yellow in autumn.

Small reddish-brown to black flower buds without petals appear before the leaves form. They expand

CAUTION: The plant has caused dermatitis in some people. Little information is available about the safety of ash for pregnant and lactating women.

The leaves also were a remedy for obesity and leprosy, as well as jaundice, kidney and bladder stones, flatulence, warts, ringworm, gout, and rheumatism.

The tree also has a mystical side. For one thing, ash has a connection with the wizard Merlin. Also, in Scotland, people ate the leaves so that when they dreamed, they would discover their destinies and the identity of their future spouse. Others believe that putting the leaves beneath your pillow is a way to induce prophetic dreams.

Habitat and Distribution: Native to Europe and western Asia. The tree grows along river banks or in mixed forests.

Growth: Deciduous tree. The plant flowers in April or May, and its seeds ripen around September to January. The leaves bud around May or early June, and stay on the trees until October. Trees begin to flower from seed when they are around twenty-five or forty years old, and they can live around 200 or 250 years, with some trees living 500 years or more. Ash prefers full sun and moist, well-drained loam soils. It can tolerate sea exposure and pollution, but is intolerant to shade or dry soil.

Origin of Earthly Fire

A legend says that God hurled a thunderbolt after Adam, Eve, and Satan when the Lord banished them from Eden. The lightning struck an ash tree, which immediately caught fire, a precious gift to humanity. Ash is one of the trees from which a "living fire" is still made. Dry wood is taken from an ash that has a trunk the thickness of a hand. The tree must also not have been planted; it must have grown on its own. Some Slavs have a saying: "The ash tree is near, everything burns." This refers to the fact that in these cultures, the people are prohibited from planting the tree near their homes because whatever is near the tree has the potential to burn (Agapkina, 182).

Curing Warts with Ash

An old superstition says that you can cure warts with the help of an ash tree. First, you'll need a new pin for each wart you want removed. Stick the pins into the tree, then prick each wart with a different pin. After removing the pins, stick them back into the tree while reciting a charm: "Ashen tree, ashen tree, / Pray buy these warts of me" (Botanical.com).

Harvesting: Fruits, seeds, bark, and leaves are used. Harvest leaves in June. Dry and store them in an airtight container. Collect the bark in spring. Dry it and grind it into a powder. Gather the seeds when they are green, including the wings. You can store them for around twelve months if you harvest them when they are ripe.

Medical Use: The leaves are primarily used in modern and traditional medicines, but bark has been an application as well. They are treatments for constipation, fluid retention, bladder problems, arthritis, gout, fever, jaundice, and rheumatism. Ash also has properties that inhibit bacteria and fungi growth, which makes it good for treating wounds and reducing swelling.

Rituals and Magical Use: Ash is a tree of protection. Carving a solar cross from ash and carrying it with you when you travel by sea is one way people protect themselves from drowning. Ash also protects the home if you hang a wooden staff over the doorposts, because the wood wards off evil. You can also scatter the tree's leaves in all directions around your home to protect it. Planting an ash tree in front of your home also provides the family with protection. It additionally has the benefit of making sure those living in the house maintain integrity. If they don't, things may not go well for them.

Like the ancients, Slavs have beliefs about snakes and ash, and the wood and leaves were used to repel snakes, and to deter the dragon zmey from capturing maidens. People believed that pouring even one drop of juice from an ash tree into a snake's mouth would kill it.

On Midsummer's Day, people blocked cracks in the home and barn with ash branches to keep snakes outside. A decoction made from ash and oak twigs was made on Good Friday and consecrated on Palm Sunday. It was then sprinkled around the yard and on the buildings to keep snakes away. Additionally, on Palm Sunday, ash wood was tossed into wells to prevent evil spirits from residing there.

It's believed that lightning never strikes the ash tree. The reasoning behind this is that the dragon zmey, with his brilliant, iridescent skin, is a zoomorphic symbol of lightning. Since, in some cases, dragons evolved from snakes, he (and therefore lightning) would avoid the ash tree.

The tree has magical healing powers as well. To prevent illness, place ash leaves in a bowl of water by your bed before you sleep. Make sure you discard the water every morning, then add fresh water and leaves to the bowl the next night. Burning ash wood at Yule is a way to receive prosperity.

Bulgarians say the ash tree brings happiness. It's also a tree sung about in Christmas carols as one that banishes demons. A person can safely rest under the the tree's shadow of the ash tree without fear of evil beings.

An old saying about ash, "Oak choke, Ash splash," says that if oaks leaf first, then the weather will be dry and dusty. On the other hand, if ash produces leaves first, the weather will have plenty of rain. In earlier days, ill children were believed to be cured if passed through the trunk of an ash sapling that had been split.

Other Use: Ash is an ornamental tree that is planted along streets. The wood tends to rot when coming in contact with soil and water. It's more suited to indoor used for veneers, garden tools, and gymnastic equipment. The creamy-white to light-brown color makes it popular for furniture making and flooring. Its wood is a good source of fuel, as even the green wood burns well.

The bark is used for dyeing, producing black, brown and green-toned dyes. The tree also has tannins and is used in tanning. The leaves are used for livestock fodder.

The ash's unripe seeds are pickled by steeping them in salt and vinegar and then used as food seasoning. In addition, an edible oil is produced from the seeds. Leaves can be used to make tea, and the young shoots are an addition to salads. The flower can be mixed with yeast and will produce a soft drink after it ferments.

Other Names: Ash, common ash.

Aromatic: The bark is bitter.

SOURCES

Agapkina, Tatyana Alekseevna. "Деревья в славянской народной традиции: Очерки." [Trees in the Slavic folk tradition: Essays.] Indrik: Moscow, 2019. https://www.academia.edu/45107661/Деревья_в_славянской_народной_традиции_Очерки.

Botanical.com. "Ash." https://botanical.com/botanical/mgmh/a/ash--073.html.

Cunningham, Scott. *Cunningham's Encyclopedia of Magical Herbs*. Llewellyn: Woodbury, MN, 2012.

European Trees. "Ash, *Fraxinus*." http://www.european-trees.com/ash.html.

Konstantinova, Daniela. "Trees that Bulgarians venerate most." December 26, 2015. https://bnr.bg/en/post/100635118/trees-that-bulgarians-venerate-most.

Missouri Botanical Garden. "Fraxinus excelsior." https://www.missouribotanicalgarden.org/PlantFinder/PlantFinderDetails.aspx?taxonid=282928.

Petrova, Bilyana, Dr. "Ясен, Планински ясен, Европейски ясен." [Ash, Mountain Ash, European Ash.] April 8, 2010, updated November 1, 2022. https://medpedia.framar.bg/ботаника/ясен.

Plants For A Future. "Fraxinus excelsior - L." https://pfaf.org/user/Plant.aspx?LatinName=Fraxinus+excelsior.

UK Safari. "Mystery Fruits on Ash Trees!" http://www.uksafari.com/ash_tree_fruit.htm.

Whitehurst, Tess. *The Magic of Trees*. Llewellyn: Woodbury, MN, 2021.

WALNUT
Juglans regia

Juglans regia
Walnut

You've probably heard an old wife's tale or two that predicts the weather. Among the Bulgarians, walnuts are one of these weather forecasters. If the crop of nuts is plentiful, expect a harsh winter. And if it thunders on St. Elijah's Day, expect a light harvest of walnuts.

Description: The walnut tree grows to a height of around 80 to 130 feet (25 to 40 meters). The crown is dense and irregular-shaped, spreading to around 65 feet (20 meters). Dark-gray bark covers the tree.

Smooth, shiny leaves have three to four pairs of leaflets, with a terminal one. Leaves turn yellow in autumn.

The tree bears both male and female flowers. The males are drooping catkins, while the females are smaller and found at the tips of the branches. When pollinated, the flowers produce a fleshy green shell. This falls off when the fruit is ripe, leaving a brown shell containing a nut that's divided into two parts.

History and Traditions: The genus name comes from the Latin *Jovis glans* or "Jupiter's nuts," and the specific name is Latin for "royal." This designation comes from the belief that in the Golden Age, men lived upon acorns, while the gods ate walnuts. The word "walnut" itself comes from an Old English word, *wealhhnutu*, which means "foreign nut," and various common names of the nut indicate its supposed origins, such as Persian walnut.

In Greek mythology, Dionysus turned Princess Carya into the tree after she died of sorrow. Historically, Pliny says the tree came from Persia. The tree is one of the oldest known, living hundreds of years, and

CAUTION: Some people have life-threatening allergies to the nuts.

even up to 1,000. As such, it was sacred. Stories say Moses's scepter was carved from a walnut tree in the Garden of Eden, and St. Patrick's scepter was made of walnut wood. Babylon priests forbade common people from eating walnuts to prevent the food from stimulating their thinking.

Throughout history, a popular belief was that foods resembled the parts of the body they cured, and so, the walnut, which looked like a brain, was treatment for that organ. In addition to the brain, the walnut is heart-shaped in the middle, and so was a remedy for heart-related problems. Walnuts were also associated with fertility and were thrown at weddings to encourage pregnancy.

All parts of the walnut tree have also been used for dyeing throughout the ages, and well-known painters (Leonardo da Vinci, Raphael, Titian, Goya, Rembrandt) mixed thickened walnut oil with their colors.

Habitat and Distribution: Native to areas from the Balkans to the Himalayas. The tree grows in warm, humid locations and can be found on mountain slopes from 1,700 up to 7,000 feet. It is widely cultivated throughout Europe. Another variety,

---

The Death of Carya

On a trip to Laconia, Dionysus, the Greek god of wine, fell in love with Carya, one of King Dion's three daughters. She felt the same toward him. Fate, or jealousy, interfered, and Carya's sisters spied on the god and gossiped about him. Enraged, he drove the girls crazy before he turned them into rocks. When Carya discovered her sisters' fate, she died of sorrow. Aggrieved himself, Dionysus turned her into a walnut tree (AgriCorti).

Waiting on the Dead

Bulgarians have numerous beliefs about walnuts. They are part of many rituals and superstitions. In particular, on Pentecost, women put walnut leaves on the graves, since they give peace to the dead during the forty days they travel the world before finally entering the other world. The women also take walnut twigs to the church service that day and kneel on them, as they believe this enables them to talk with their deceased loved ones. Another belief is that by touching your ear to the trunk of a walnut tree, you can talk to those who have passed on (Bulgarian Heritage Team).

Juglans nigra (black walnut), is more popular in North America.

Growth: Deciduous tree. The buds appear mid-April to late-May, and the leaves fall in early November. Flowers blossom before the tree is in full leaf. Fruits ripen in autumn. Trees grown from seed will produce fruit in eight to twelve years, while grafted cultivars take five years to produce fruit. Walnut trees grow in deep, rich, well-drained soil with full sunlight. Its deep root system helps it resist droughts, but it's susceptible to frost damage.

Harvesting: Leaves and bark are used for medicinal purposes. Strip off leaves singly in June and July while the tree flowers. Do it in the morning after the dew has evaporated. Dry them outside in half-shade. When drying leaves and bark indoors, select a warm, sunny room with a temperature of 70 to 100°F (21 to 38°C). Leave a window or door open so air circulates. Spread the leaves and bark in a single layer without them touching, and turn them as they dry. Store dried parts in airtight containers in a dry place. Leaves retain their color when dried.

Medical Use: In medicine, walnut leaves have disinfectant and anti-inflammatory properties, while the bark is a remedy for parasitic worms. Treatments are for irregular menstruation, eczema and skin infections, diarrhea, inflamed gums, osteoporosis, and more. Walnut remedies are believed to help with appetites, tone the nervous system, and promote the growth of bones and connective tissues.

In folk medicine, a decoction from the leaves is applied externally to rinse wounds and skin diseases, eye inflammation, hemorrhoids, and measles. In addition, rubbing the liquid into the scalp and combing the hair helps prevent hair loss.

Studies from the nineties have shown that walnuts lower cholesterol and reduce heart damage after a heart attack.

One of Bach's Thirty-eight Flowers, walnut is used as protection from change and unwanted influences. Although the person may be fulfilling his own ideals and not seeking the opinion of others, on occasion, he may turn away from his own beliefs because of being easily influenced by the enthusiasm of others.

Rituals and Magical Use: Walnuts are a symbol of longevity and generosity. Bulgarians have a tradition that finding a plump nut inside the shell on Budni vecher (Christmas Eve) means you'll be healthy and successful for the year. On the other hand, the tree has connections with illness and death. If the nut is shriveled inside its shell, you'll suffer illness and have bad luck. Healers, however, have a way around the bad luck. They'll toss walnuts around and say, "As the walnuts are scattered, so the *uroki* [evil spirits] are scattered and go away."

Healers also have a treatment where they rub boils with walnuts, then throw the nuts at the crossroads. Any person who finds the discarded nuts and takes them away, also takes the disease with them.

In various cultures, including Bulgarian belief, it's considered dangerous to sleep within the tree's shadow. Anyone doing so will be overcome by

disease, because this is where Samodivi, woodland nymphs, gather. This concept possibly comes from the fact the tree produces a toxic substance that harms other plants (although not humans).

Sometimes, however, the Samodivi aren't causing mischief to those seeking shelter in the thick shade. An Easter song tells how a shepherd sheltered his flock there from the scorching sun. The only problem was that not all the sheep fit within the bounds of the shade. A Samodiva came and extended her wing to provide a shadow for those outside. In return, the shepherd played his *kaval*, shepherd's pipe, for her.

Among the Bulgarians, it was detrimental to plant a walnut tree, because it was believed the person would die when the trunk was as thick as the planter's neck. To prevent this, the person laid a long red belt in a circle on the ground, creating a magic circle, and planted the tree in the center. The human's life would pass naturally before the tree trunk reached the circle.

In Italy, it was believed that witches danced beneath walnut trees while the women performed secret rites.

Other Use: Walnut is a healthy snack, raw or cooked. All parts of the walnut tree can be used to create dyes from golden to brown. The wood is durable and used for flooring and furniture. Walnut oil makes a good wood polish. Painters apply it as a varnish and use it as a medium for mixing colors. Walnut leaves are also a good substitute for moth balls.

Other Names: Common walnut, Persian walnut, English walnut, Carpathian walnut, Madeira nut.

Aromatic: The leaves produce a lemon or lime scent when crushed. Leaves and bark have a bitter, astringent taste. The walnut has a rich flavor.

SOURCES

AgriCorti. "The Walnut Tree in Greek Mythology." https://www.agricorti.it/en/il-noce-nella-mitologia-greca/.
Alfrey, Paul. "The Essential Guide to Everything you Need to Know about Growing Walnuts – Juglans regia." November 23, 2016. https://www.permaculturenews.org/2016/11/23/essential-guide-everything-need-know-growing-walnuts-juglans-regia/.

Aviva. "Dyeing with the walnut tree and more!" October 29, 2021. https://thefoxandtheknight.com/walnut-tree-dyeing/.

The Bach Centre. "Walnut." https://www.bachcentre.com/en/remedies/the-38-remedies/walnut/.

Bezovska, Albena. "Green walnut tree growing." April 19, 2015. https://bnr.bg/en/post/100546558/green-walnut-growing.

Botanical.com. "Walnut." https://botanical.com/botanical/mgmh/w/walnut06.html.

Bulgarian Heritage Team. "Орехът в българския бит и култура." [The walnut in the Bulgarian way of life and culture.] May 21, 2017. http://bgnasledstvo.org/bg/орехът-в-българския-бит-и-култура/.

Cunningham, Scott. *Cunningham's Encyclopedia of Magical Herbs*. Llewellyn: Woodbury, MN, 2012.

Iliev, A.T. "Растевеята отъ българско фолклорно гледище." [Plants from the Bulgarian folklore point of view.] Historical and Philological Journal, May 18, 1916. http://parks.bg/wp-content/uploads/2016/07/11.-Iliev-At.-Rasteniyata_ot_bylgarskoto_folkorno_gledishte.pdf.

Mikhailova, S., Dr. "Шепа орехи или „празник за ума"." [A handful of walnuts or a "feast for the mind."] https://kenguru.bg/shepa+orehi+ili+%E2%80%9Epraznik+za+uma%E2%80%9D/1/MlW-gRSXMhSvMxOvU5WfcJSvYJODM1e3YhOzcVOzgleDUJePg9KbQpaHgta-INirMpWLQtiLcZmrYp.

Online Etymology Dictionary. "Walnut (n)." https://www.etymonline.com/search?q=walnut.

Petrova, Bilyana, Dr., ed. "Орех, Обикновен орех." [Walnut, ordinary walnut.] March 25, 2010, updated on January 26, 2020. https://medpedia.framar.bg/ботаника/орех-обикновен-орех.

Whitehurst, Tess. *The Magic of Trees*. Llewellyn: Woodbury, MN, 2021.

BAY LAUREL
Laurus nobilis

Laurua nobilis
Bay laurel

The common name of this plant brings two thoughts to mind. First, "bay" evokes images of sauces simmering on the stove, a bay leaf adding its flavor to the other spices, while an enticing fragrance fills the kitchen. Second, "laurel" brings forth images of ancient athletes battling to wear the victory crown, and as such, it is symbolic of victory and success.

Description: Bay laurel can grow between 33 and 60 feet (10 to 18 meters), but normally will reach heights of 10 to 30 feet (3 to 9 meters). It can be pruned to 8 feet (2.5 meters) or smaller for a garden.

It has a pyramidal or rounded shape and spreads to 5 to 20 feet (1.5 to 6 meters). The plant's bark is smooth with an olive-green or reddish hue.

Shiny, dark-green, lance-shaped leaves are thick and leathery. Their edge is smooth and wavy. The leaves alternate up the twig on short stalks.

Small yellowish-green flowers are both male and female, but only one type blossoms on the plant. The flowers grow in clusters. Pollinated flowers on the female plant produce a shiny purplish-black fruit that contains a single seed.

History and Traditions: The genus name is the Latin name for the tree and had the meaning of "verdant," because of the green coloring of the leaves. Its Latin origin is uncertain. The "L" in Latin often corresponds to the "D" in Greek and Proto-Indo-European, making

CAUTION: The spice can interact with various pain medications and sedatives. Adequate studies of the herb for medicinal use have not been undertaken, so pregnant or lactating women should not use or use with caution, as well as anyone with blood sugar problems.

the word *"daurus."* This may be connected to the Greek *daphne* (as in the mythology story), or the word *"daurus"* may be the original word. This is related to the Indo-European root *deru* for "tree." The specific name is Latin for "noble," "notable," or "excellent." The common name of "bay leaf" is derived from the Latin *bacca* for "berry," which originally referred to the plant's fruits.

In western mythology, the tree is most familiar in relation to the ancient Greek story about the nymph Daphne and the god Apollo. In one version of the tale, Apollo had been struck by one of Eros's love arrows, while Daphne a hate one. In order to avoid Apollo's romantic intentions, Daphne was turned into the laurel tree either by herself, by the earth goddess Gaea, or by Daphne's father, Peneus. Thereafter, Apollo wore wreaths made from the laurel as a reminder of the love she didn't share with him.

Victors of the Pythian Games, which were dedicated to Apollo, were crowned with the highly esteemed laurel wreath. The wreath was a sign of high status, and emperors, generals, and poets were also known to wear one. Under the influence of the Pythian Games, as early as 776 B.C., the winners of the Olympic Games changed from being crowned with a wreath of olive twigs in honor of Zeus to being crowned with laurel.

The leaves were also considered sacred. Delphic priestesses chewed them and inhaled their fumes when burned as incense. This helped put them into

---

Acne Remedy

If you suffer from acne, try this natural tonic using bay laurel. Boil 5 g of the leaves in a cup of water for about 5 to 6 minutes. Apply the liquid twice daily to your skin. Or place a warm compress on your face daily. Use four leaves for every 4 cups (1 liter) of water (Petrova).

Wrinkle Reduction

Well-known herbalist Petar Dunov has a recommendation for reducing wrinkles. Boil five leaves in 300 ml of water for 10 minutes. Whip three egg whites until foamy. Mix 15 ml of olive oil with the bay leaf decoction. Beat the mixture well, then add 10 g of alum. Apply the mixture to a piece of velvet cloth and place it on your face overnight (Petrova).

a prophetic state of mind. The laurel also symbolizes Christ's resurrection in Christianity.

Medically, the leaves in the past were treatments for hysteria, flatulence, colic, and other problems. Additionally, they were used for inducing abortions. And ancient Egyptians thought the leaves would cure hangovers.

Habitat and Distribution: The tree grows in the Mediterranean area, although it probably originated from Asia Minor. Its habitat is woodlands and thickets.

Growth: Broadleaf evergreen tree or large shrub. Although the plant has leaves year-round, the flowers bloom between March and May. It prefers full sun or partial shade and rich, moist, well-drained soils. Bay laurel can tolerate strong winds, but not frosts.

Harvesting: Leaves, fruit, oil, and bark of young branches are used. Oil can be extracted from the fruit and leaves. Leaves dry quickly after being picked and don't need exposure to sunlight. The best leaves have a bright-green color and a strong aroma. They should be kept for one year, at most, in an airtight container somewhere dark. Discard them after a year, because they become brown, lose their fragrance, and gain a bitter taste.

Medical Use: The leaves not only add flavor to food, but they also boost fiber, vitamins, minerals, and antioxidants. When the herbs are taken in large doses, the chemical compound lauroside from the tree helps inhibit cancer cell development. The fresh leaves also have enzymes that trigger the production of insulin. Bay laurel additionally helps improve cardiovascular health, thereby reducing the risk of heart disease.

Drinking tea made from the leaves is a means to ease an upset stomach or calm nerves, and its aroma helps relieve sinus problems. An oil from the fruit can be made into a salve to treat sprains and bruises, itching and mild skin irritations, as well as relieve pain as an ear drop. For head and chest cold relief, simmer the berries and leaves until they're soft and make a poultice of them before placing them on the chest.

A decoction made from ten leaves boiled for an hour in about 4 cups (1 liter) of water is one way to help with hair loss. Cover your hair with the liquid, then wrap it in a towel for an hour, before washing it from your scalp. Try it also for dandruff and greasy hair.

Rituals and Magical Use: One of bay laurel's magical abilities is its power of protection. When worn as an amulet, bay laurel wards off negativity. If you're looking for protection from lightning, place the leaves on the windowsills.

Poltergeists will behave if you hang bay laurel around your home. Burning the leaf during an exorcism ritual also aids in removing more troublesome evil. To remove curses, burn leaves that have been mixed with sandalwood. You can also plant a tree near your home to protect your family from sickness.

Bay laurel also gives the user psychic powers. Placing the leaves under your pillow while you sleep will enable you to have prophetic dreams, while burning the leaves will give you visions. You can even make your wishes come true by writing them on the leaf, then burning it.

Healing is another power of bay laurel leaves. A wreath of the leaves can be worn while a healer treats an ill person. This increases the power of the spell while it protects against negative energy. Once the sick person has recovered, burn the leaf to purify the room.

Other abilities of bay laurel are keeping love permanent; providing athletes strength; giving a person confidence, direction, and focus; bringing prosperity and wealth; protecting people from harassment; and enabling them to be seen in the world in the way they want to be seen.

Other Use: The leaves of the bay laurel have been a spice at least since the days of ancient Romans. Use in cooking is still the most popular application of the herb, especially for soups, stews, sauces, fish, and meats, where it's left in the dish before heating to absorb its flavor. Most often, you'll find it as a dry leaf, but it's also used fresh and as a powder. The fruits can be used in spice mixes and are best used in sauces and gravies.

Other than being used as food, the plant contains essential oils that make it suitable for aromatherapy, where it helps alleviate migraines and headaches, reduce muscle and joint pains, and ease the pain of arthritis.

The oil is also an ingredient in cosmetics, perfumes, and soap. Because of the strong fragrance of the dried leaf, it's added to potpourri, wreaths, and other crafts; used to deter moths in closets; and added to a bag of flour to keep bugs out.

Additionally, the plant is ornamental, decorating gardens and creating low hedges. Bay laurel is resistant to pests and diseases, and it protects nearby plants as well. Due to its strong aroma, it makes a good insect repellent.

Other Names: Bay tree, true laurel, sweet bay, royal bay, Turkish bay leaf, daphne, laurel, Grecian laurel, Roman laurel, poet's laurel, victor's laurel, noble laurel.

Aromatic: The wood has a sweet scent. The fresh leaves release a pine-like scent when bruised, and they are quite bitter, but drying them reduces the bitterness and improves the flavor. The dried fruits have a similar aroma, with a robust taste.

SOURCES

Botanical.com. "Laurel (Bay)." https://botanical.com/botanical/mgmh/l/larbay10.html.

Cunningham, Scott. *Cunningham's Encyclopedia of Magical Herbs*. Llewellyn: Woodbury, MN, 2012.

Gernot Katzer's Spice Pages. "Laurel (Laurus nobilis L.)." http://gernot-katzers-spice-pages.com/engl/Laur_nob.html.

Missouri Botanical Garden. "Laurus nobilis." https://www.missouribotanicalgarden.org/PlantFinder/PlantFinderDetails.aspx?kempercode=d418.

Morningbird. "Bay Laurel: Folklore, Healing & Magical Uses." October 29, 2019. https://witchipedia.com/book-of-shadows/herblore/bay-laurel/.

Petrova, Bilyana, Dr. "Дафиново дърво, Лаврово дърво." [Bay tree, Laurel tree.] April 9, 2010, updated on November 30, 2022. https://medpedia.framar.bg/ботаника/дафиново-дърво-лаврово-дърво.

Plants For A Future. "Laurus nobilis - L." https://pfaf.org/user/plant.aspx?LatinName=Laurus+nobilis.

Pollux, Amaria. "The Magickal Properties of Bay Leaves." https://wiccanow.com/magickal-properties-of-bay-leaves/.

WebMD Editorial Contributors. "Bay Leaf: Health Benefits, Nutrition, and Uses." Reviewed on December 11, 2022. https://www.webmd.com/diet/bay-leaf-health-benefits.

Whitehurst, Tess. *The Magic of Trees*. Llewellyn: Woodbury, MN, 2021.

APPLE
Malus domestica

Malus domestica
Apple

⚠️

If any fruit should be called magical and mystical, it's the apple. It's been popularized as the fruit involved in the fall of mankind from grace in the story of Adam and Eve in the Garden of Eden. And who can forget the adage "An apple a day keeps the doctor away." An even older version of the saying exists: "To eat an apple going to bed / Will make the doctor beg his bread." Not least of all, is the magical experience of autumn apple-picking. This sweet, delectable fruit has many more uses as well.

Description: In the wild, apple trees can grow up to 30 feet (9 meters), while cultivated trees are more likely to be around 16 feet (5 meters) tall, with a dense crown, spreading 15 to 25 feet (4.5 to 7.5 meters). The bark is gray, and the twigs are initially downy.

Dark-green leaves are elliptical with jagged edges, and the underside has a light moss covering. They alternate up the twig. In autumn, the leaves turn red and brown.

Deep-pink buds become pale-pink or white after they fully open. The flowers have five petals. They blossom at the same time as the leaves bud. The fruits are oval-shaped and can be red, green, or yellow. Seeds are contained within five cavities that form a star shape.

History and Traditions: The genus name is the Latin for the apple. Its accusative form, *malum*, was thought to have been confused with *mălum*, meaning "evil" (from the neuter accusative form), thus making the apple the forbidden fruit in the

CAUTION: The seeds, and possibly the leaves, contain hydrogen cyanide. Eating large quantities of the seeds can make breathing difficult or cause spasms. They may even result in a coma or death.

Garden of Eden. The specific name refers to the fact it is a domesticated species. The common name of "apple" comes from the Proto-Indo-European *ab(e)l-*, but its original meaning is uncertain. Up until the late seventeenth century, the word "apple" was generically used for all fruits except berries.

The apple tree is one of the oldest plants to be cultivated. It has around 7,500 known varieties. The fruit has been used for medical treatments for centuries. Hippocrates used it to treat heart and kidney disease.

Apples have also played a role historically and in mythology. Newton's discovery of gravitation occurred after he saw an apple fall from a tree. In Greek mythology, another apple caused all sorts of problems, the apple of discord, on which was written "to the prettiest one." Paris had to decide which goddess attending a wedding should receive the fruit. His choice of Aphrodite offended Hera and Athena. Things spiraled out of control, and the result was the Trojan War.

The Forbidden Fruit

The fruit of the tree of knowledge of good and evil that Adam and Eve were commanded not to eat from is commonly portrayed as an apple. However, the fruit is only described as *peri*, a general word for "fruit." Historians say it could have referred to any number of fruits, including pomegranate, fig, grape, pear, quince, or mushroom.

How did the apple become this forbidden fruit?

A couple of thoughts seem to prevail. One is that it comes from John Milton's *Paradise Lost*, in which he calls the fruit an apple. Another belief is that the association with apple occurred when the Bible was translated into Latin, since the word *malus* can mean "apple" or "evil" (Compassion.com).

Habitat and Distribution: Originating in central Asia, the plant is now widely cultivated through much of the northern hemisphere. In warmer climates, it can be found in mountainous areas.

Growth: Deciduous tree. Apples blossom from April to June. They produce mature fruit in late summer or autumn, normally 120 to 150 days after flowering, depending on the variety. With some varieties this can be as little as 70 days or as long as 189 days. Trees that are three to five years old start producing fruit. Commercial varieties most often are grafted onto other rootstocks, since they don't grow well from their own roots. The plant needs full sun to attain the maximum fruit production, and it grows best in loamy, well-drained soil.

Spiced Apples

To make spiced apples, select and peel ones that have a firm shape. For every 3 pounds of apples you have, use 1 quart of vinegar, 4 pounds of sugar, 1 ounce of cinnamon stick, and 0.5 ounce of cloves. Boil the ingredients, then add the apples. Cook the apples until they're tender, then put them in a jar. Continue to boil the liquid until it forms a thick syrup. Pour this over the apples and cover them. Keep them in a cool place for up to a few months (Botanical.com).

The fruit contains quercetin (which stimulates the activity of the immune system and protects brain cells, among others), fiber (which is good for the digestive system), pectin (good for gastrointestinal problems), fatty acids (help with metabolism and digestion), vitamins (to rejuvenate the skin), boron (which helps the body absorb calcium), and flavonoids (which may help keep your pancreas healthy and reduce the risk of type 2 diabetes).

Two-thirds of the fiber is found in the skin, as well as antioxidants and other substances that help protect you against cancer, heart disease, and stroke.

Juice from apples helps eliminate harmful bacteria in the mouth, and combined with honey, helps fight colds, fatigue, depression, arthritis, and other problems. One study suggested the juice could improve mood and behavior of Alzheimer's sufferers. Eating apples helps whiten teeth and clean teeth and gums, in addition to relieving headaches.

Rituals and Magical Use: Among the Slavs, the apple tree is the tree of love and is dedicated to the goddess Lada. As such, apples play a role in Bulgarian courting and marriage rituals. At a secret *sedyanka* (half-working, half-party evening gatherings between young people), young women of marriageable age performed many rituals. The last one of the evening was to attach apples to a wooden apparatus used to wind wool and twirl it around to encourage young men to twirl around the girls. After this, the young woman would give her apple to a young man of her choice.

At weddings, an apple covered with gold foil tops the wedding banner as a sign of fertility. In addition, an odd number of apples (also covered with gold foil) are stuck into branches of the wedding tree (*kum*'s tree), which can be the crown of a small tree, a bush branch, a forked stick, or a distaff.

Other wedding customs involving apples were that an apple was placed in water in which the bridegroom washed. Afterwards, the apple was brought to the

Harvesting: Fruit and bark are used. You can store them for at least twelve months, sometimes longer. Avoid storing apples with potatoes, as the fruit will lose its flavor. And apples will cause carrots and potatoes to become bitter if stored together. To preserve apples, wrap maple leaves around them.

Medical Use: Apples are used to treat multiple problems: diarrhea, chronic constipation, anemia, insomnia, coughs, nervousness, and more. The fruit is helpful in achieving weight loss, lowering the risk of heart attacks, reducing the likelihood of cataracts, lowering blood pressure and cholesterol, reducing the risk of osteoporosis.

bride's home and placed in water she would use to wash her hair. After the wedding, the couple would eat their first official meal as a married couple at the bride's home. This could involve feeding each other apples and lumps of sugar.

Rituals with apples even continue after the wedding. In some areas, the bride is brought into a garden that has an apple tree. Three boys will throw her veil onto the tree. The woman's brother-in-law puts three red apples into a bag he brought with him that holds the bride's wedding shirt, as a symbol that healthy children will be born to her.

An apple's core forms a pentacle shape, a symbol associated with magic and pagan rites performed for the Mother Goddess. Each of the five points of this star represents the five elements: earth, air, fire, water, and spirit.

The fruit is also an ancient symbol of abundance, health, and fertility, since the pentacle signifies life and well-being. And apples are said to have the power of love. The blossoms are strained out after being added to melted pink wax. Burning candles made from this wax are used to attract love. Among the Bulgarians, an apple represents a maiden, her face ruddy and wholesome, and one who can bear healthy children like plentiful apples.

The apple's spherical shape has been equated with eternity. Consequently, apples have been a symbol of death and immortality since Adam and Eve ate the forbidden fruit in the Garden of Eden. The fruit is considered the food of the dead among various cultures. A popular Bulgarian saying is that if a person dies smiling, it means St. Michael has given him a golden apple in exchange for his soul. In Celtic mythology, a branch that had buds, flowers, and ripened fruit was magical and enabled the person who held it to enter the gods' realm and the underworld. Apples, in Norse mythology, were associated with the goddess Indun. Her apples gave other deities their immortality.

In Bulgarian folk belief, when wild apples are plentiful, people predict winter will be "evil," especially if the *Petrovki* variety ripens on October 14, St. Petka's Day. Lots of wild apples as well as hawthorn will predict a bad winter, and winter will be severe if both apples and sloes are plentiful.

Other Use: Apples make delicious treats no matter how you prepare them. You can eat them raw, cooked, or dried. Some popular dishes are jams and jellies, cider, applesauce, and pies. When apples are cut, vitamin C is lost due to oxidation. Apples stored in the refrigerator or a cool place retain the largest amounts of vitamin C, while apples that are heated have the least.

The apple tree's fine-grained wood is hard and compact. This makes it a good wood for items such as tool handles and canes. The wood also is good for fuel.

Other Names: Orchard apple. Synonym: *Pyrus malus*, called wild apple or crab-apple.

Aromatic: The blossoms have a delightful fragrance, while the fruit, depending on the variety, can range from sour to sweet and have textures ranging from mealy to crisp. The bark, in particular the root-bark, is bitter.

SOURCES

Aleksstosich. "Стабло живота – The Tree of Life." September 27, 2018. https://svilenkonac.net/2018/09/27/стабло-живота-the-tree-of-life/.

Botanical.com. "Apple." https://botanical.com/botanical/mgmh/a/apple044.html.

Compassion.com. "The Forbidden Fruit and the Origins of Poverty." https://www.compassion.com/christian-faith/forbidden-fruit.htm.

Cunningham, Scott. *Cunningham's Encyclopedia of Magical Herbs*. Llewellyn: Woodbury, MN, 2012.

Iliev, A.T. "Растевеята отъ българско фолклорно гледище." [Plants from the Bulgarian folklore point of view.] *Historical and Philological Journal*, May 18, 1916. http://parks.bg/wp-content/uploads/2016/07/11.-Iliev-At.-Rasteniyata_ot_bylgarskoto_folkorno_gledishte.pdf.

MacDermott, Mercia. *Bulgarian Folk Customs*. London and Philadelphia: Jessica Kingsley Publishers, 1998.

Missouri Botanical Garden. "Malus domestica 'Co-op 38' GOLDRUSH." https://www.missouribotanicalgarden.org/PlantFinder/PlantFinderDetails.aspx?taxonid=265825&isprofile=0&pt=7.

Nedelcheva, Anely and Yunus Dogan. "Usage of plants for weather and climate forecasting in Bulgarian folk traditions." *Indian Journal of Traditional Knowledge* 10, no. 1 (January 2011): 91-95. https://www.academia.edu/12909328/Usage_of_plants_for_weather_and_climate_forecasting_in_Bulgarian_folk_traditions.

Online Etymology Dictionary. "Apple (n.)" https://www.etymonline.com/search?q=apple.

Petrova, Bilyana, Dr. "Ябълка." [Apple.] April 8, 2010, updated November 1, 2022. https://medpedia.framar.bg/ботаника/ябълка.

Plants For A Future. "Malus domestica - Borkh." https://pfaf.org/user/Plant.aspx?LatinName=Malus+domestica.

RxList.com. "Diet and Nutrition: The Health Benefits of Apples." Reviews on February 4, 2021. https://www.rxlist.com/health_benefits_of_apples_diet_and_nutrition/article.htm.

V., Stefan. "The Cult Of The Trees in Slavic Mythology." https://www.slavorum.org/the-cult-of-the-trees-in-slavic-mythology/.

Whitehurst, Tess. *The Magic of Trees*. Llewellyn: Woodbury, MN, 2021.

ORIENTAL PLANE
Platanus orientalis

Platanus orientalis
Oriental plane

Image: Vinayaraj, CC BY-SA 3.0 <https://creativecommons.org/licenses/by-sa/3.0>, via Wikimedia Commons.

This magical plant is considered sacred by many. I, too, have experienced the wonder of the tree when I visited the home of the beloved Bulgarian prophetess and healer Reverend Stoyna (1883–1933) in Zlatolist, Bulgaria. A 1,300-year-old plane tree grows in the middle of the yard. People leave folded pieces of paper in its trunk and tie the red-and-white *martenitsi* charms onto its branches, because a legend says the tree can perform miracles, and those who stand beneath its crown will be healed.

Description: The plane tree typically grows to around 60 to 80 feet (18 to 24 meters), while some may reach a height of 120 feet (36 meters). It has a dense, round to pyramidal-shaped crown that spreads to 50 to 70 feet (15 to 21 meters). When growing in the open, it branches a few feet above the ground and develops into several large, spreading limbs. Young shoots are greenish-brown and covered with gray or pale-brown hairs. If the side branches are trimmed, the tree forms a straight trunk. Its grayish-brown bark peels and flakes. The bark may also develop deep cracks like scales of a snake. As the tree ages, it often becomes hollow.

Dark-green leaves have five to seven deeply cut lobes, with the ones at the side being smaller. They are lance-shaped with one to three large teeth or smaller lobes. Thick, whitish-brown hairs cover the leaves when they first unfold, but later fall off. The leaves alternate and tend to grow horizontally. In autumn, the leaves turn yellowish-brown or orange.

Flowers are greenish and round, growing in clusters of two to six to a stalk. They produce bristly, spherical fruit balls that turn brown when ripe. They contain 500 to 600 seeds. The fruits continue to grow into early winter.

History and Traditions: The genus name comes from the Greek *platus* for "large" or "broad," and the specific name is Latin for "eastern."

A plane tree that is more than 600 years old was the winner of the Bulgarian tree of the year in 2010 and came in second place as the European tree of the year. These trees can live from 500 to 2,000 years.

The plane tree was the second most prized tree of antiquity, coming in behind the cedars of Lebanon. Ottomans planted a plane tree near water whenever they conquered a new land. This signified they had the right to rule that location.

This ancient tree figures into Greek mythology. It's symbolic of regeneration because its bark flakes off and regrows. The plane tree is another species from which the Trojan horse was said to be made, and the tree is elsewhere described in the *Iliad*; beneath its

---

CAUTION: The hairs on the fruits and leaves cause an effect similar to hay fever.

branches was a place where Greeks made great sacrifices before sailing off to Troy.

Plane trees were planted near monasteries. Other mentions of the tree include a reference to Hippocrates teaching medicine beneath one on the island of Kos. A sprout from this tree is still said to be alive there. Pliny talks about a plane tree under which was held a dinner party for eighteen staff members. It was also a favorite tree for people to meet or rest because its branches kept out the hot rays of the sun.

Habitat and Distribution: Native to southeastern Europe and western Asia. The tree grows around riverbanks, and you can find them growing on or next to large rocks that overhang streams.

Growth: Deciduous tree. The flowers bloom between March and May, and the seeds ripen from October to February. It needs full sun and cannot grow in deep shade, although it will tolerate light shade. The best soil is rich, moist, and well-drained. Once the plant is established, it is drought tolerant and can withstand strong winds and pollution.

Harvesting: Leaves and bark are used. Harvest them in spring and summer. Dry them and store them in a cool place.

Medical Use: In folk medicine, oriental plane leaves can be bruised and applied to the eyes to treat inflammation and conjunctivitis, while a cream made from the leaves helps heal wounds and scarred skin. Other uses are for treating skin problems, gastrointestinal issues, rheumatism, knee

---

Breeding Jacob's Spotted, Speckled Flocks

You may be familiar with the Bible story in which Jacob uses peeled bark in the water to influence the breeding habits of the flock. His goal was to produce livestock with stripes, speckled, or spots, or whichever appearance his father-in-law, Laban, deemed to be Jacob's current share. Even though Laban initially removed all the animals that met Jacob's suggested wage, Jacob still managed to produce the desired offspring. Was this a magical, divine, or natural event?

It's been hypothesized that even though the animals were not speckled, spotted, or striped, there were some among them that had a genetic trait to produce this type of offspring, since there had been some originally among the flock, before Laban took them away. According to the Bible, Jacob saw this in a dream, so he knew which animals to breed.

Jacob peeled sticks, exposing the white streaks, and placed them in the animals' watering places. It was here that the flocks bred. Sticks from plane trees were one of those that he used (as well as poplar and almond), and their medicinal properties were best extracted when the wood was in water. Therefore, it's possible that the reason behind placing the peeled sticks in the water was to ensure the herd was healthy (Lacey).

pain, and inflammation. Boiling the bark in vinegar is a treatment for diarrhea, hernias, dysentery, and toothaches. The fruit is also believed to help eliminate wrinkles.

Rituals and Magical Use: The tree represents greatness, permanency, superiority, and sovereignty. It's also believed that the tree helps pregnant women have a successful delivery, while it protects others from infertility. To ensure this health, women tear out colored strips from their dresses and tie them to the tree's branches.

When a plane tree appears in your life, it means you should be objective and impartial, seeking fact-based truths when it comes to people who need advice or help. The tree is telling you to use your intellect rather than emotions when you advise others. Seeing a plane tree may also mean you need to pursue higher education or use what you already know in a new way. It's time to be intellectual and expand your worldview.

Other Use: The tree's most popular use is as a shade tree. Other uses include making dyes from its branches and roots, and the wood is used in making furniture, cabinets, crates and barrels, instruments, plywood, and butcher blocks. It's also believed that plane trees help purify the air and repel plague and other airborne diseases.

Other Names: Oriental plane tree, oriental sycamore, chinar. Synonym: *Platanus vulgaris*. The trees are called planes in British English and sycamores in American English. The name "sycamore," however, has also been used for *Ficus sycomorus* and *Acer pseudoplatanus*.

Aromatic: The tree has a sweet, balsamic aroma, which becomes stronger when you handle the leaves.

SOURCES

Browicz, Kazimierz. "On the geographical distribution of *Platanus orientalis* L. in Bulgaria." *Arboretum Kórnickie* 9 (1964). https://rcin.org.pl/Content/141966/KOR001_145864.pdf.

The Encyclopedia of Diderot & d'Alembert. "Plane tree." https://quod.lib.umich.edu/d/did/did2222.0002.280/--plane-tree.

European trees. "Plane tree." http://www.european-trees.com/oriental-plane.html.

Goreme1990. "Turkish symbolism – meanings found in trees, graveyards and flowers." February 2, 2021. https://www.insideoutinistanbul.com/turkish-symbolism/.

Irtiza, Syed, Gulzar A. Bhat, et al. "Antioxidant and Anti-inflammatory Activities of *Platanus orientalis*: An Oriental Plant Endemic to Kashmir Planes." *Pharmacologia* 7, issue 4 (2016): 217-222. DOI: 10.17311/pharmacologia.2016.217.222. http://docsdrive.com/pdfs/pharmacologia/2016/217-222.pdf.

JungleDragon. "Platanus orientalis." https://www.jungledragon.com/image/9234/platanus_orientalis.html.

Lacey, Troy. "Jacob's Odd 'Breeding Program' of Genesis 30." April 26, 2019. https://answersingenesis.org/genetics/animal-genetics/jacobs-odd-breeding-program-genesis-30/.

Missouri Botanical Garden. "Platanus orientalis." https://www.missouribotanicalgarden.org/PlantFinder/PlantFinderDetails.aspx?kempercode=d263.

Music of the Plants. "Music of the Plants - Platanus orientalis in the garden of Prepodobna Stoyna, Bulgaria." June 28, 2016. https://www.youtube.com/watch?v=FZUNFq29y5Y.

Plants For A Future. "Platanus orientalis - L." https://pfaf.org/user/Plant.aspx?LatinName=Platanus+orientalis.

Rix, Martyn, and Michael F. Fay. "857. PLATANUS ORIENTALIS: Platanaceae." *Curtis's Botanical Magazine* 34, no. 1 (2017): 29–40. https://www.jstor.org/stable/48505732.

The Spirit Wisdom. "Plane – Counsel." https://treespiritwisdom.com/tree-spirit-wisdom/plane-tree-symbolism/.

Tree-guide.com. "Oriental Plane Tree." http://www.tree-guide.com/oriental-plane-tree.

Trees and Shrubs *Online*. "Platanus orientalis l." https://treesandshrubsonline.org/articles/platanus/platanus-orientalis/.

OAK

Quercus robur

Quercus robur
Oak

You'll often hear the oak called majestic. It's a magical, sacred World Tree for many cultures, connecting the heavens, earth, and underworld through its branches and roots. Not only does it connect the physical realms, but it also connects the creatures who inhabit them. In cosmogonic myths, an iron oak holds water, fire, and earth, and its roots rest on divine power.

It is through the World Tree that the universe is kept in balance. Sacred ceremonies were held beneath its branches, and the holy place was called an *obrok*. In later times, people paid respect to the saints here, and sick people slept beneath the tree's branches to get well.

Description: This species of oak belongs to the white oaks. Depending on its location, the mighty, majestic oak reaches an average height of anywhere between 40 to 115 feet (12 to 35 meters) and older trees up to 130 to 165 feet (40 to 50 meters), with a spread of 40 to 70 feet (12 to 21 meters).

The crown starts low on the trunk and is symmetrical and round or oval, with a smooth outline. Lower branches are more pyramidal when young. Young branches are bare and rigid, while older trees have thick grayish-brown to black cracked, furrowed bark.

Short-stalked, oblong leaves alternate along the twig and vary in size. They have three to seven rounded lobes on each side. The upper side is a shiny dark green, with a lighter, almost blue-green color underneath. They turn a coppery color in autumn. Dry leaves may persist on the tree throughout winter and only give way to new buds in spring.

> **CAUTION**: May cause digestive problems or delay absorbing alkaloids and other alkaline drugs. Pregnant and lactating women should avoid use due to lack of information on its safety.

Small yellowish-green flowers blossom on catkins. Females produce oval acorns, with up to four on a stalk. The raw acorns are light green, becoming a shiny brown as they ripen. Acorns have a cap that connects them to the stem.

History and Traditions: The genus name comes from the Celtic *quer* for "fine" and *cuez* for "tree." And *robor* is from the Latin word for "robust," due to the tree's strength and durability. The word "durable" itself comes from *duir*, the ancient Celtic word for the oak. The word "oak" is thought to have originated from the Proto-German. And in Indo-European languages, the word "oak" sometimes referred to trees in general.

Oaks were sacred to the Druids, who performed ceremonies in groves where the trees grew. The word "druid" can be translated to "oak knowledge," "oak-knower," or "oak-seer," and represents the holy men's knowledge and wisdom. Oak was also a holy wood among the Romans, who, according to legend, burned the wood in their Vesta fires.

The wood of the oak also served practical needs. Because of its strength and durability, it was used to build ship hulls until the mid-nineteenth century. In addition, it was used to create barn beams, barrels,

railroad ties, flooring, and furniture. Tannin in the bark has also been used to tan skins throughout the ages.

Ten thousand years ago, before wheat was cultivated, acorns were ground to make flour. Among early Native Americans, acorns were held in

---

Budnik Ceremony

A three-year-old oak was chosen for the *budnik*, or in some countries, only a branch from the tree was cut. Before the man cuts the tree, he begs it or the spirits and fairies who live there, for forgiveness. Out of reverence for the tree and spirits, the man makes sure the tree doesn't touch the ground when it's cut.

Back at home, ritual words are spoken about the "Young God" whose spirit inhabits the tree as the man brings the god into the home. The log is placed by the hearth to be blessed and anointed with wine, olive oil, and incense, which are poured into a hole made on the thicker end and then plugged. The log is burned the entire night, transforming into the living figure of the Young God as the body of the old god burns.

The ceremony doesn't end there. The ashes are considered magical and healing. They are used in medical treatments and are also scattered on fields, vineyards, and meadows to protect them and make them fertile (from our book *Light Love Rituals*).

such importance that the people were called "acorn-eating" tribes.

Habitat and Distribution: Native to Europe and western Asia, growing in mixed woodlands and lowlands, along rivers, and in foothills and mountains. It is widely distributed to other areas, such as North America, northern Africa, and scattered throughout parts of China.

Growth: Deciduous tree. Catkins appear around the same time as the foliage emerges in April or May, and acorns ripen around mid-autumn. Oaks can tolerate a variety of soils, but they prefer moist, well-drained loam soils. They also prefer full sun. Mature trees can withstand flooding and drought.

Oaks are slow-growing trees. A tree may reach twenty-five to forty years of age before it produces acorns, and even up to sixty years before it yields a full crop. Once they start bearing nuts, oaks produce smaller crops for two years and a large one in the third year, which is a means of preventing animals like squirrels from eating the entire crop each year. Instead, the animals will hoard the nuts (often forgetting where they hid them in the ground), and so new trees can grow.

The trees also have long lives, living in some cases more than 1,500 years, like one tree in the Stara Zagora region in Bulgaria. Once the oak reaches 100 years, its growth slows, increasing by less than an inch a year.

Harvesting: Branch bark and acorns are used. Collect the bark from young trees in early spring when the tree's juices are moving the strongest, and dry it in the sun. Gather acorns once they have fallen from the tree.

Medical Use: Remedies using oak are for a variety of skin conditions, such as eczema, cracked skin, pimples, and itching. It's also been a treatment for hemorrhoids, diarrhea, stomach inflammation, and heavy menstruation. Other uses are for gingivitis, tonsillitis, bad breath, and cold sores. Oak has also been used as an antidote for alkaloid poisoning, to stimulate the appetite, and as an anti-inflammatory. To relieve inflammation from stings, cuts, or bites, lay a bruised leaf over the injury.

Ritual Fortunetelling

Oak is also used in a ritual divination called extinguishing live coals. The woman performing the ritual pours water from a spring into a green clay dish. Neither the water nor dish have been used for any other purpose. She submerges a sacred quartz, crystal, or rock into the water, then stirs the water with a stalk of basil and cuts through the water three times with a ritual knife while she recites an incantation each time. Finally, with her hands or with tongs, she picks up three, seven, or nine live oak coals and, one by one, tosses them into the water.

Each coal represents one of the questions the person who has come to see her has asked. Three things will provide the answer: the sound the coal makes when it touches the water, whether the coal floats or sinks, and if it floats, the direction it moves in. If the coal sizzles a long time, the answer is a positive outcome. If the sizzle is weak and short, or if the coal sinks, the result will be misfortune. If the coal floats east or south, the results will be positive.

The coals and water both become sacred with magical powers. If the person seeking their fortune is sick, they will wash with the water. Someone bewitched will drink it and blacken themselves with the coals, or even make them into an amulet (Ristic, 161-164).

Oak is another one of Bach's Thirty-eight Flowers. The remedy is administered to people suffering from overexerting themselves with work and those who can't stop before they reach their goal. The elixir helps them to admit they are exhausted and realize they need to rest.

Rituals and Magical Use: Oak is a tree of power. It represents inner strength, wisdom and knowledge, vitality and life, healing and health, protection, money and luck, and thunder and weather. You can channel the tree to use earth or weather magic. Oaks were used for transference of pain into the tree, which could endure the temporary ailment before sending it into the earth through the tree's roots or into the sky through its branches.

As with other tree rituals for healing, people would walk around an oak three times. In some cases, the sick person would speak to the tree and ask its advice, as in the case of a person desiring to relieve a toothache. "Tell me, tell me, my beloved oak tree, how should I treat my teeth?" Mentioning the oak in their chants was not necessary, however. What was important was to be near the tree and receive its healing power.

A story tells how a girl gained powers after sleeping beneath an oak. Witches had predicted that the girl would destroy someone she loved. The girl confessed this publicly and was redeemed from the curse. However, after that, she became ill for three years, so she went to sleep beneath an oak. She dreamed a man showed her how to heal livestock with herbs. When she awoke, she was healthy, but she noticed sick cattle nearby. With her newfound knowledge, she cured them and then went on to become a cattle healer.

Oak twigs have been used as charms against evil. Burning oak leaves will purify an area, and burning an oak log will carry away sickness. Acorn charms help retain youth or gain fertility. Acorns on a windowsill are believed to protect the home against

lightning, and planting an acorn during a full moon is done for prosperity.

The oak (for a boy) and birch (for a girl) are called upon in a charm to get a crying child to go to sleep. "Oak, oak, you are black! You, oak tree, oak trees have sons, and birch trees have daughters. You, oak and birch, make noise and thicken, and the born child (name) sleep and grow!"

Oak trees are more likely to be struck by lightning than most other trees. This has to do with their high water content and the fact they are commonly the tallest plants in the areas in which the trees grow. Among the Slavs, oak is revered as the tree of Rod,

the father of the gods, and Perun, their supreme god, deity of the sky and thunder. When thunder struck a person's home, it was believed Perun was protecting the family from Volos, the god of the underworld. This god had escaped and disguised himself as a serpent and had hidden himself within the home. A similar belief is that the female demon or dragon Ala or Hala lived in oak trees. Lightning strikes the trees, attempting to kill her.

It was taboo to cut the tree down for fear misfortune would befall the person or even his home and village. The exception to cutting the oak was Christmas Eve, when the wood was burned as the *budnik* or Yule Log. Even then, special rites were performed.

Animal spirits are believed to protect the tree at night. And the eagle and dragon *zmey* both perched on its branches to keep watch over the fields. During droughts, people sprayed the oak with holy water to keep it safe, and the people prayed for rain as they gathered around an oak. In addition, field workers wore oak twigs around their waists to keep them safe during the harvest.

Oak is another weather predictor in Bulgarian folk belief. When the tree produces many acorns, winter will be severe and snowy. In addition, food will become expensive. An abundance of acorns, cornel fruits, and hazelnuts also is a prediction of a severe winter.

Other Use: Oak makes a good shade tree. It also remains a popular tree for ship-building and construction. Artists find it a good wood to carve despite its immense strength. And it's good as a fuel, burning slowly and providing great heat.

Bark from the oak is used for tanning leather and creating dyes, and you can mix powdered bark with peppermint oil to make a toothpaste. Additionally, an infusion made from oak bark is good to treat greasy hair.

You can eat the acorns, but you should leech the tannic acid from them first. Then you can eat the nuts or grind them into flour. Chopped and roasted acorns are an almond or coffee substitute. The ground nuts are a good thickener for stews. An edible gum from the bark can be used in place of butter for cooking.

Other Names: Common oak, pedunculate oak, European oak, English oak, black oak, French oak, Polish oak, Slavonian oak.

Aromatic: Acorns are bitter if eaten raw, due to the tannic acid. Powdered bark as part of an herbal tea also has a strong, bitter taste, but is somewhat aromatic.

SOURCES

Agapkina, Tatyana Alekseevna. "Деревья в славянской народной традиции: Очерки." [Trees in the Slavic folk tradition: Essays.] Indrik: Moscow, 2019. https://www.academia.edu/45107661/Деревья_в_ славянской_народной_традиции_Очерки.

Botanical.com. "Oak, Common." https://botanical.com/botanical/mgmh/o/oakcom01.html.

Dana. "Sacred Tree Profile: Oak's Medicine, Magic, Mythology, and Meanings." Updated on April 17, 2022. https://druidgarden.wordpress.com/2018/11/11/sacred-tree-profile-oaks-medicine-magic-mythology-and-meanings/.

Eco Enchantments. "The Magic of the Ogham Trees." https://web.archive.org/web/20210610083223/http://www.ecoenchantments.co.uk/myogham_oakpage1.html.

Gilman, Edward F. and Dennis G. Watson. "Quercus robur – English Oak." Fact Sheet ST-558, October 1994. https://hort.ifas.ufl.edu/database/documents/pdf/tree_fact_sheets/queroba.pdf.

Israfela. "How is the cosmos perceived according to the Bulgarian folk belief?" February 18, 2018. https://wiccanrede.org/2018/02/how-is-the-cosmos-perceived-according-to-the-bulgarian-folk-belief/.

Kilgore, Georgette. "Oak Tree Guide: 7 Types, Colors, Leaves, Identification (How to Buy, Plant)." December 6 2022. https://8billiontrees.com/trees/oak-tree/.

Konstantinova, Daniela, trans. "Make-up on a white face, lipstick on thin lips." December 6, 2013. https://bnr.bg/en/post/100274812/make-up-on-a-white-face-lipstick-on-thin-lips.

MacDermott, Mercia. *Bulgarian Folk Customs*. London and Philadelphia: Jessica Kingsley Publishers, 1998.

Malyuta, A. N. "Священные деревья древних славян." [Sacred trees of the ancient Slavs.] August 16, 2016. https://zvezdakrama.org/svyashhennye-derevya-drevnih-slavyan.

Missouri Botanical Garden. "Quercus rubra." https://www.missouribotanicalgarden.org/PlantFinder/PlantFinderDetails.aspx?kempercode=i760.

Nedelcheva, Anely and Yunus Dogan. "Usage of plants for weather and climate forecasting in Bulgarian folk traditions." *Indian Journal of Traditional Knowledge* 10, no. 1 (January 2011): 91-95. https://www.academia.edu/12909328/Usage_of_plants_for_weather_and_climate_forecasting_in_Bulgarian_folk_traditions.

Petrova, Bilyana, Dr., ed. "Дъб обикновен, Летен дъб." [Oak, Summer Oak.] April 15, 2010, updated on February 21, 2020. https://medpedia.framar.bg/ботаника/дъб-обикновен-летен-дъб.

Plants For A Future. "Quercus robur - L." https://pfaf.org/user/Plant.aspx?LatinName=Quercus+robur.

Ristic, Radomir. *Balkan Traditional Witchcraft*. Los Angeles: Pendraig Publishing, 2009.

Stavreva, Lilia. *Български магии и гадания*. [Bulgarian magic and divination.] Trud Publishing House: Sofia, 2007.

Trees for Life. "Oak mythology and folklore." https://treesforlife.org.uk/into-the-forest/trees-plants-animals/trees/oak/oak-mythology-and-folklore/.

V., Stefan. "The Cult Of The Trees in Slavic Mythology." https://www.slavorum.org/the-cult-of-the-trees-in-slavic-mythology/.

BUCKTHORN
Rhamnus frangula

Image: Kommentator1989, CC BY-SA 4.0 <https://creativecommons.org/licenses/by-sa/4.0>, via Wikimedia Commons.

Rhamnus frangula
Buckthorn

Buckthorn is like a shy child, standing at the corner of the playground, with head lowered, away from all the rambunctious activity. It believes you feel it has nothing special to offer the world. Although it may not be a majestic World Tree or produce a delectable fruit, just the fact buckthorn is a tree makes it worthy of admiration. Buckthorn provides nectar for bees and leaves for caterpillars before they become the beautiful butterfly. The tree stands there, wanting to be appreciated and become your friend.

Description: This shrub or small tree can reach a height of up to 23 or even 49 feet (7 to 15 meters). As a shrub, it grows to around 10 feet (3 meters).

The plant's bark is cinnamon-black, but as it ages, it turns silver-gray to gray-brown to dark gray, or even black. The inner bark is a bright lemon-yellow.

Elliptical, smooth-edged leaves have a shiny dark green color on top and yellow-green underneath, and they alternate up the twig. Unlike other buckthorns, this variety lacks thorns. The leaves turn yellow in autumn.

Star-shaped flowers with five petals are small and greenish-white and grow in clusters of two to ten. They produce green berries that turn red, then black or black-violet when ripe and contain two or three roundish seeds.

History and Traditions: The genus name comes from the Greek *rhamnose* for "branch," and the specific name comes from the Latin *frangere* for "to break," because the wood is brittle.

CAUTION: Fresh bark and berries are poisonous and will cause severe vomiting. Avoid long-term use of dried bark, as it will lose its laxative effect and can intoxicate the body, causing diarrhea, dehydration, and weakness. Do not use if pregnant, lactating, or having abdominal pain. Always consult a medical professional before using.

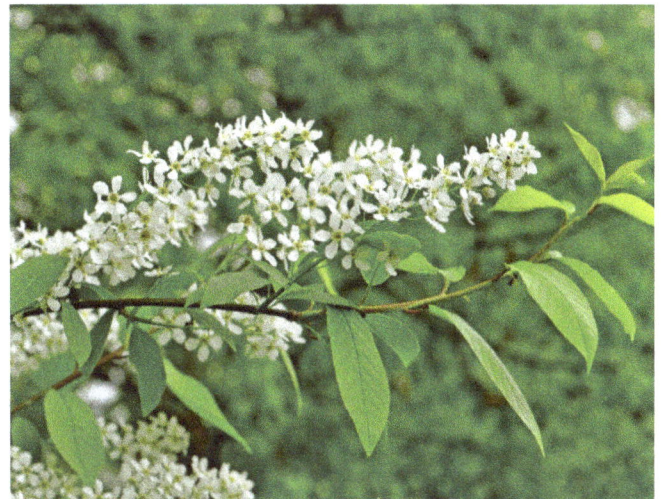

The plant has been used as a gentle laxative since the Middle Ages or earlier. It was also used for tanning at one time. In addition, buckthorns were believed to protect against witchcraft and demons, as well as poisons.

Distribution and Habitat: Native to Europe, northern Africa, and western Asia, and naturalized in North America. It grows in open woodlands, near rivers and other damp places, and in mountainous regions.

Growth: Deciduous tree or shrub. The plant blooms from May through July, and the fruit ripens from September to November, depending on the location. Buckthorn can also grow in many soil types, sandy, loamy, clay, but thrives in wet, peaty soil, with full sunlight or moderate shade, but not deep shade. Keep the plant watered, but not water-logged, and keep it out of strong winds. Sucker roots travel underground to produce new plants.

Harvesting: Bark is used, but it must be dried for *at least one year* before using, because fresh bark is poisonous and violently purgative. In spring, before the leaves sprout, strip bark from the trunk or moderate-sized branches from a plant that's at least

---

Ritual for De-hoarding Your Home

It's easy to collect too much "stuff." But then how do you go about getting rid of unwanted possessions? It can be an overwhelming task. Here's a ritual to help you along.

Place a half dollar at the base of a buckthorn tree. Show respect to the tree and ask to cut off part of a branch in return. Walk through each room of the house, waving the branch in a counterclockwise sweeping motion to purify the area. When you're finished, lay the branch on the ground, to return it to the earth.

With the air clear of negativity, you can now begin the process of decluttering. Start with a small area, even just a cupboard. You'll find you have more ambition to do it and finish the tasks until your entire house is clutter-free (Isabella).

three years old. Dry the bark outside in half shade on a sunny day, or inside on trays in a heated, well-ventilated room.

Medical Use: Only dried bark should be used in treatments. Even then, using it excessively can be dangerous. It should be administered for short-term, occasional application. European studies covering a period of at least ten years have provided scientific evidence of the effectiveness of the herb. Buckthorn increases muscle tone and muscle contractions in the digestive track, and so it acts as a gentle laxative that works within six to ten hours after taking.

External use in folk medicine is for oozing wounds, jaundice, boils, scalp infections, and other skin diseases. A treatment for scabies calls for soaking the fruits in vinegar for twenty days before applying it to the skin.

Rituals and Magical Use: Amulets made from the bark and berries will bring wealth. Branches placed around a home's windows and doors will drive away evil sorcerers. And if you have legal problems, carry a piece of the bark with you when you go to court for good luck. Having a piece of the bark with you is also a good talisman for any kind of new endeavors and to keep you motivated and confident. Another use of buckthorn is to make a wand from a branch for healing. It's the tree that picks the person, not the other way around, and it can be stubborn about its choice.

Other Use: The plant attractis butterflies. It was once grown for use as charcoal to make gunpowder. Now, artists use it for drawing. The bark and leaves produce a yellow dye, the unripe berries a green one, and ripe berries a blue or gray dye.

Other Names: Alder, black dogwood, frangula bark, glossy buckthorn, breaking buckthorn.

Aromatic: The bark has a sweet, slightly bitter taste. It'll turn your saliva yellow.

SOURCES

DBotanical.com. "Buckthorns." https://botanical.com/botanical/mgmh/b/buckth80.html#com.

European Medicines Agency. "Frangula bark." November 20, 2019. https://www.ema.europa.eu/en/documents/herbal-summary/frangula-bark-summary-public_en.pdf.

Isabella. "The Magickal Buckthorn Tree." April 23, 2020. https://speakingofwitchwands.net/2020/04/23/the-magickal-buckthorn-tree/.

Petrova, Bilyana, Dr., ed. "Зърнастец, Франгула, Горска зърника, Бабушка, Дива боя, Чернилка." [Buckthorn, Frangula, Forest Grain, Grandma, Wild Paint, Chernilka.] March 30, 2010, updated on January 7, 2021. https://medpedia.framar.bg/ботаника/зърнастец-франгула-горска-зърника-бабушка-дива-боя-чернилка.

Plants For A Future. "Rhamnus frangula - L." https://pfaf.org/user/Plant.aspx?LatinName=Rhamnus+frangula.

Wand More. Question from tangygoose-blog. https://wandmore.tumblr.com/post/169596434575/hello-would-you-analyze-the-frangula-buckthorn.

SMOKETREE
Rhus cotinus

Rhus cotinus
Smoketree

An image of beauty with its wispy flowers, smoketree is a plant that should inspire myths about its origins. It compels you to imagine a Daphne-type character, fleeing a god's love, or perhaps a Narcissus, admiring his own beauty. Then, by the will of the gods or the person's own choice, transformation begins, and an exquisite new plant species is born.

Description: This multi-branched shrub or small tree with an irregular shape grows to a height of around 12 to 20 feet (3.5 to 6 meters) and a width of 10 to 15 feet (3 to 5 meters). The smooth branches are reddish to brown, and the bark is light gray or yellow.

The plant's rounded leaves have a waxy sheen and alternate on the twigs. They are dark green on top and bluish-green underneath, with a reddish tinge, but turn yellow, orange, and red in autumn.

Numerous pink to cream flowers cluster together. After they blossom, the stalks grow and are covered with yellow-pink, pink-purple, or red-violet hairs, making them look like a haze or puffs of smoke. Smoketree produces dry, dark-brown fruits.

History and Traditions: The genus name comes from the Greek *rhous* for "sumac." The specific name and

CAUTION: The herb should not be ingested. Using it as a mouth rinse without swallowing is considered safe. Internal use can cause intoxication. Use under medical supervision.

the older genus name come from the Greek *kotinos* for "wild olive tree."

Historically, the tree has been used to make a dye for clothing because of the chemicals in its sap. The color, however, was quick to fade. During the Civil War, the plant almost became extinct from over-harvesting. It's still used in Europe for its tannin content.

Habitat and Distribution: Native to southeastern Europe and Asia. A variation of the plant, *Cotinus obovatus*, grows in North America and may have been introduced because of nineteenth-century trade with China. It's found in forests and rocky locations with poor soil.

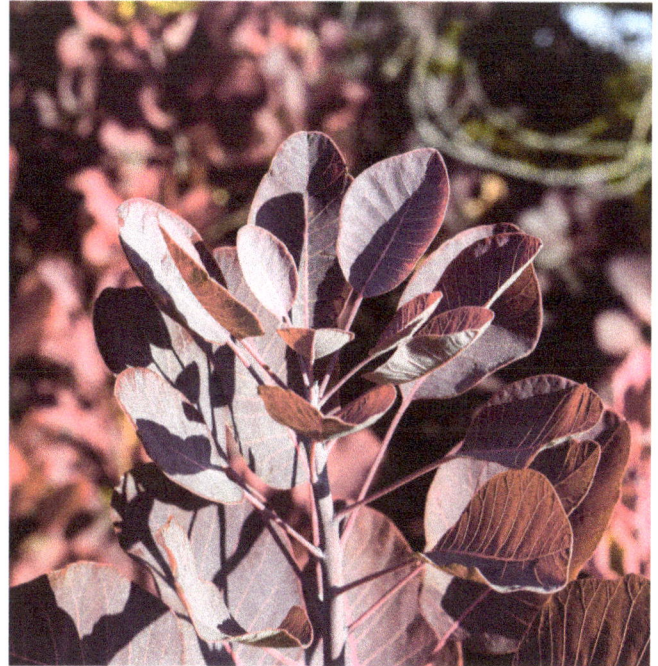

Growth: Deciduous shrub or small tree. The plant blossoms around May or June. It can tolerate a range of soils, from light and sandy to wet, heavy clay, and it grows in partial shade or full sunlight.

Harvesting: Leaves and bark are used. Harvest them after the shrub flowers, before the fruit forms. Dry the parts in the shade, in a well-ventilated room, or

---

Skin Treatment with Smoketree

Oily Skin: Add 1 Tablespoon of smoketree leaves and 1 Tablespoon of thyme into 0.5 liter of boiling water. Strain the mixture through a fine sieve after 10 to 15 minutes. Allow the decoction to cool before using it to cleanse your face. It's good to apply the decoction after a steam bath.

Pigment Spots: Mix equal amounts of smoketree leaves, fennel seeds, and oatmeal with one part olive oil. Stir until it's uniform. Apply to pigment spots for 20 minutes, then wash off with lukewarm water.

Inflamed Gums: Mix 1 teaspoon of smoketree leaves, 1 teaspoon of chamomile, and 1 teaspoon of baking soda. Dissolve in 1 liter of water. Boil on low heat for around 5 minutes. Strain the mixture and rinse your gums (Bilki.bg).

in a dehydrator at up to 122°F (50°C). Stir and turn them during the beginning of the drying process. After drying, remove the large stems. Store the herbs in bags in a dry, ventilated place. When pruning the bush, wear old clothing, because the stem juice is sticky and can stain.

Medical Use: This herb is applied externally for skin diseases as an anti-inflammatory and antiseptic, such as for acne, pimples, wounds, frostbite swelling, feet sweating, hemorrhoids, boils, and gingivitis. The yellow bark can also be steeped and used as a coagulant, fever reducer, or eye ailment treatment. Investigation into applications of Bulgarian plants determined the herb has antioxidant capabilities greater than those of black or green teas.

Rituals and Magical Use: The tree is a tool for spiritual and emotional cleansing. A person can relax beneath the branches on a sunny day for personal cleansing, while the tree does its magic of removing negative energy, unhappiness, and misfortune from the surroundings.

Other Use: Smoketree is an ornamental plant. A dye can be made from the roots and stems, and the leaves and bark are a source of tannins, so the plant has been used in the leather, dyeing, and perfume industries. The leaves are steam-distilled and the extract used as an ingredient in shampoos, toothpastes, food flavoring, wine, and tobacco.

Other Names: Smoke tree, smoke bush, European smoketree, young fustic, wig tree. Synonym: *Cotinus coggygria*.

Aromatic: The fresh and dried leaves have a characteristic smell and tart taste. When crushed, they smell like orange peels.

SOURCES

Bilki.bg. "Смрадлика, тетра, действие и приложение на билката." [Smoketree, tetra, action and application of the herb.] https://bilki.bg/encyclopedia-bilki/smradlika-tetra.html.

European Trees. "Cotinus either Smoke tree." http://www.european-trees.com/smoke-tree.html.

ISSG (Invasive Species Specialist Group). "Cotinus coggygria." http://www.iucngisd.org/gisd/species.php?sc=1174.

Othman, Sheereen. "Smoketree: A Mystic Mirage." August 3, 2020. https://arbordayblog.org/treeoftheweek/smoketree-mystic-mirage/.

Petrova, Bilyana, Dr., ed. "Смрадлика, Тетра." [Smoketree, Tetra.] March 25, 2010, updated on August 25, 2021. https://medpedia.framar.bg/ботаника/смрадлика-тетра.

Whitehurst, Tess. *The Magic of Trees*. Llewellyn: Woodbury, MN, 2021.

BLACK LOCUST
Robinia pseudoacacia

Robinia pseudoacacia
Black locust

Older trees may lack these thorns. The leaves turn yellow in autumn.

White clustered flowers produce a brownish bean-like fruit, with dark brown seeds. The tree spreads through underground shoots.

History and Traditions: The plant's genus is named after royal French gardeners, Jean Robin and his son, who introduced it to Europe in 1601. The specific name comes from the Greek *pseudo* for "fake" or "false," and *acacia*, referring to the species of plants.

The wood is resistant to rot for up to 100 years. Historical folklore says it helped Americans win the War of 1812 because their ships used locust nails, compared to the oak ones on the British ships (which caused the ships to fall apart more easily during cannon fire). The wood was also used to build structures in Jamestown during the height of colonization.

It's said that lightning strikes this tree more than any other. In historical times, the tree was associated with the vernal equinox and symbolized the deification of the sun, rebirth, immortality, and new beginnings due to its vitality and endurance. In addition to renewed life, it symbolized platonic love among the peoples of the Mediterranean countries. People believed the tree was sensitive to touch, especially if its flowers or twigs were torn off.

Habitat and Distribution: Native to North America, but it's also found in southern South America, Europe, northern and southern Africa, Australia, New Zealand, and Asia. It thrives in cooler climates.

Growth: Deciduous tree. It flowers from May to June. The plant grows best in fertile soils and full

Every rose has its thorn, and the same could be said of the black locust tree. And like the rose, this prickly plant produces a side benefit that makes people admire and endure its ability to hurt: the sweet honey made from its flowers.

Description: The tree reaches an average height of 82 feet (25 meters), with a spread of 30 to 50 feet (9 to 15 meters). Its crown is narrow and its bark cracked and grayish-brown, forming diamond-shaped patterns. Branches jut out at odd angles, and the overall appearance of the tree is scraggly.

Rounded, blue-green leaves are dark on top and have a lighter underside. The paired leaves have short thorns protruding at the base of the stem.

CAUTION: The bark, leaves, and wood are toxic to both humans and livestock. The flowers are considered safe in small doses, but may cause nausea, vomiting, and headaches with a larger intake. Use only with a doctor's supervision.

sunshine. Because black locust tolerates pollution, it's planted in parks, along roadsides and railways, as well as in private yards and gardens.

Harvesting: Leaves, bark, flowers, and fruits are used. In May and June, pick blossoms with a yellow center. Brown ones are past their prime. Use blossoms fresh or dry them in the shade in a ventilated place without direct sunlight, or dry at 104°F (40°C) in a dehydrator. Once they're dry, store them in paper bags or cardboard boxes for up to one year.

Medical Use: The leaves, bark, and fruits are used in folk medicine, but because they are poisonous, must be taken only with medical supervision. Tea made from the blossoms is used as an expectorant, to lower a person's temperature or inflammation of the urinary tract, and to lessen symptoms of the flu

and coughs. Historically, the plant has been used as a laxative and to suppress muscle spasms, as well as to reduce high blood pressure, ease stomach pain, and help stop internal bleeding. A hot drink made from the twig bark helps with ulcers, heartburn, and constipation. Acacia honey is light-colored and has a pleasant aroma. The honey helps alleviate digestive and respiratory diseases.

Rituals and Magical Use: Since the plant is a new world tree, not much has been written about its magical uses. It's associated with endurance,

---

Black Locust Tea

Add 1 Tablespoon of dried black locust flowers to 300 ml boiling water. Leave the soaked flowers in a covered porcelain or glass container for about 2 hours, then filter the tea. Drink small portions throughout the day (Ivanov, 84).

Sweet Treat – Jam

Boiling the flower petals with sugar produces a light, sweet, perfumed jam.

60 g of acacia blossoms
1 kg of brown sugar
1 packet of lemon juice

Use only the petals. Rinse and boil them in 0.5 liter of water for 10 minutes. Add sugar and continue to boil. Add the lemon juice before removing from the heat and stir until dissolved (Todorova).

black locust stick (perhaps a splinter) into a person's skin. Failure to remove it could cause the infected person to die. People make ritual combs and hair pieces from the thorns. It's been suggested that, in America, it can replace the blackthorn for magical powers.

Other Use: Since it's a hardwood tree, its wood is used in flooring, furniture, fence posts, and other projects that require a durable product. The tree is planted for erosion control and to provide sandy soil with nitrogen. But it's considered invasive in many locations since it crowds out grasslands.

Essential oil from the flowers is an ingredient in perfumes and toiletry waters and a spice in sherbets. Acadia honey is made from its flowers, and the blossoms are edible, being made into jams, meads, wines, or added to salads.

Other Names: False acacia, white acacia, white salkum.

Aromatic: Blossoms are fragrant and taste like fresh sweet peas.

strength, and power and has a connection between life and death, looking dead itself most of the time, while simultaneously restoring life to the land. In this way, it may help the living get in touch with the dead.

Some sources say the thorns were believed to repel evil forces and can also be used in piercing spells. One way to enact a curse was to put a sharpened

---

SOURCES

Blood and Spicebush. "The Folkloric Uses of Wood Part VII: Black Locust." July 9, 2016.
   http://www.bloodandspicebush.com/blog/the-folkloric-uses-of-wood-part-vii-black-locust.

The Druid's Garden. "Sacred Tree Profile: Black Locust's Medicine, Magic, Mythology and Meanings." https://druidgarden.wordpress.com/2019/11/10/sacred-tree-profile-black-locusts-medicine-magic-mythology-and-meanings/.

Ivanov, Ivan Isaev, Prof.; Iliya Ivanov Landzhev, Dr. of Pharmacy; Geo Kirilov Neshev, Dr. of Medicine. *Билките в България и използването им.* [Herbs in Bulgaria and their use.] Zemizdat: Sofia, 1977.

Lekuva.net. "Какво се лекува с цвят от бяла акация?" [What is treated with white acacia?] May 3, 2014. https://lekuva.net/62645/kakvo-se-lekuva-s-tsvyat-ot-byala-akatsiya.html.

Petrova, Bilyana, Dr., ed. "Бяла акация, Бял салкъм." [White acacia, White salkum.] March 16, 2010, updated on August 13, 2021. https://medpedia.framar.bg/ботаника/бяла-акация-бял-салкъм.

Todorova, Ani. "Бялата акация – нещо различно, полезно и вкусно." [White acacia – something different, useful and delicious.] May 14, 2018. https://purvite7.bg/byalata-akatsiya-neshho-razlichno-polezno-i-vkusno/.

WHITE WILLOW
Salix alba

Salix alba
White willow

⚠️

30 meters) and having a spread of 40 to 70 feet (12 to 21 meters). The tree is upright, and its branches form a wide, rounded but irregular, leaning crown. The trunk's dark-gray to gray-brown bark develops deep cracks as it ages, while the willow's gray-brown to green-brown shoots are straight, slender, flexible, and brittle. Silver hairs cover young twigs, but drop off as the twig develops. Branches turn brown, gray, green, red, or yellow in winter and have narrow buds near the twig.

Narrow oval leaves with a finely serrated edge run consecutive along the twig and have short stalks. Fine, silvery hairs cover the leaves all over, but lose most of the downiness on the top as the leaves grow. In autumn, the leaves turn pale yellow.

White willow flowers on a single tree are either all male or all female, so both are needed in order to obtain seeds. The male catkins are showier than the females, with tiny yellowish antlers while females have small greenish flowers. When pollinated, female catkins grow longer and develop many small capsules that have a grassy green color. Inside are many tiny seeds that are enclosed in a white down. When the capsule is ripe, it cracks.

History and Traditions: The Latin genus name comes from the Proto-Indo-European *sal(i)k-* for "willow," with the specific name being the Latin for "white."

White willow bark has been used medicinally for thousands of years among the Chinese. Additionally, medical uses have been discovered among the writings of Sumer, Assyria, and Ancient Egypt, right up to the present. It was particularly well-known as the first source of salicylic acid, an ancient-day

There's something calming and romantic about willows. Paler than most other trees in the species because of the fine, white hairs on the underside of the leaves, the white willow drapes its slender, flexible branches toward the water, providing shelter for wildlife. Beneath its shadow is a cool place to sit and reflect about life and the world, while listening to the branches rustle in the breeze.

Description: White willow is the largest of the willows, growing to a height of 50 to 100 feet (15 to

CAUTION: White willow should not be used by pregnant and lactating women; those suffering from asthma, stomach ulcers, kidney or liver disease, or diabetes; those who have allergies to aspirin; or anyone taking medication to lower blood pressure. If taken in large doses, the herb may cause gastrointestinal bleeding, kidney damage, nausea, rash, dizziness, or mouth sores.

aspirin, and used to relieve joint pain and reduce fevers.

Habitat and Distribution: Native to Europe, northern Africa, and central and western Asia. European settlers brought it to the U.S. in the 1700s, where it has since become naturalized in North America. It grows in wet, poorly drained areas, such as near rivers, streams, lakes, marshes, and swamps.

Growth: Deciduous tree. Flowers and leaves appear between March and June, and the seeds mature around June. The plant prefers full sun, but it can grow in partial shade but not full shade. It does best in moist soils. The tree can withstand pollution. White willows grow fast and should be permanently planted as soon as possible. They have a short life due to being prone to disease and insects.

Harvesting: Bark, leaves, and shoots are used. The bark can be used fresh or dried. It's best to gather it from the branches of trees that are three to six years old, as this is when the sap movement is most intense. It's also easy to extract the bark from the tree throughout summer. Dry bark in small pieces and store them in a dry place. Harvest stems in spring or summer. Remove the leaves and steam the stems to strip out the fibers.

Medical Use: White willow bark has been a medical treatment since ancient times. A folk remedy to cure sick people was to crush willow leaves and smear

the juice on the patient's face. If the juice turned red, it meant the person would live. If instead it turned yellow or black, they believed the person would die. A more practical remedy is to make a tea with the bark to cure fever, coughs, headaches, rheumatism, diarrhea, and all manner of pain. Poultices can be applied to infected wounds, and a tonic drunk to purify the blood.

Other treatments of white willow products are for angina, rheumatoid arthritis, osteoarthritis, toothaches, muscle pain, skin rash, sweating feet,

---

The Fairy Healing Arts

A story is told about a man who was carried away by fairies and taught the healing arts. They gave him a willow rod to use in his practice, but was told to never charge more than a small amount to any of his patients. If he ever ran out of medicinal herbs, all he had to do to summon the fairies for more was to stand in front of his family's hearth and touch himself three times with ashes (Ristic, 48).

Origin of Pussy Willows

A tale from Poland is told about the origin of the buds of the willow, called pussy willows. A farmer was angry when a cat on his property had kittens. Not wanting to feed any more animals, he stuffed the young into a sack and threw it into the river. The mother sat crying on the riverbank, but her babies didn't return. A willow that grew nearby took pity on her and dipped its branches into the water and pulled out the sack. Unfortunately, the kittens had drowned. In honor of the mother and her lost kittens, willows everywhere burst into kitten-like buds each spring (Green, 28).

An old saying is, "Whoever plants a willow with his own hands near the house prepares a spade for himself." The meaning behind this is that when the tree is large enough for a shovel to be made from the tree's wood, the person who planted the tree will die.

In the beliefs of the Slavs, willows are a border between the world of the living and that of the dead. Swinging among the tree's branches is where you will find Rusalki, as they love to laugh and play there. These spirits of females who have drowned or died a violent death are often called mermaids because of their habit of drowning men who come too close, but these water maidens lack fish tails. From the willow's branches, Rusalki call out to passing men, enticing them to come closer. And if the men do, the Rusalki will tickle them to death. Other water spirits also sit in willows and bend the branches to the water. And the spirits of drowned prisoners sit in the trees at night.

Willows were once known as trees of celebration, but today they are associated with sadness and mourning, such as on Palm Sunday, known in Bulgaria as Vrubnitsa (Willow Day) or Tsvetnitsa (Flower Day). At a solemn Sunday service, the priest blesses and distributes willow twigs to the congregation. Each person takes this now-sacred object home. Some will place it by the family ikons, while others will wear it to protect from the evil eye or as a cure for backaches and headaches. The twig may even be buried in the garden or field to deter moles and other pests and keep hail and disasters away.

On this day, people believe that the dead can return to the human world. These spirits are not the undead, like Rusalki or vampires, but family members who have passed on and now need nourishment. One woman from each household will go to the cemetery before sunrise. She'll cense the graves, pour water and wine over them, start a fire on them, and stick a willow wand near the headstones to

heavy menstruation, internal bleeding, heart disease, insomnia, and colic.

To use as a cold remedy, soak 1 teaspoon of the bark in half a liter of cold water for 8 hours. Filter the liquid and drink once a day.

Rituals and Magical Use: Since the willow is symbolic of spring's nature, the tree is dedicated to the Slavic god Jarilo, who ushers in springtime. The tree also has an association with the serpent, because of the flexibility of the plant's shoots.

The tree symbolizes rapid growth, strength, and restorative powers. It's used in rituals to bring rain.

honor the departed. She'll also offer bread, boiled wheat, and wine to anyone else she sees in the graveyard.

A young willow tree symbolizes health and fertility. On St. George's Day (April 23), cattle and women alike are gently whipped with the branches with the belief the willow will ensure they produce offspring. Still potent after this beating, the branches are thrown onto fields to make sure they also provide a bountiful harvest. On the other hand, an old tree is called cursed. Not only for the fact it no longer provides fruit or shade but also because as it becomes hollow inside, it serves as a refuge for evil spirits.

Other customs involved whipping a person with a willow's branches to drive out fever. The reasoning behind this was that some demon had entered the person and had to be driven away. If someone didn't want the fever whipped out of him, he could roast an onion and approach a willow early in the morning. He would shake the tree three times, each time saying, "I'm not shaking away your morning dew. I'm shaking away my fever." He then left the onion under the tree and, as he departed, would say, "The fever will take me when this onion sprouts."

Shaking the tree was also a means for a person to transfer the illness to the willow. It was necessary to arrive at the tree before sunrise. As soon as the sun appeared, the person would hug the tree and say, "Let the fever shake you. Let the sun shine on me."

A sick person could also bathe in water near the tree. When they were through, they would leave a piece of clothing on the branches and not look back when leaving. Or, as an alternative, someone else would bring the ill person to sit under the tree. She then chanted, "As this tree bends, so does (the ill person's name) stand tall."

Other beliefs about willows are:

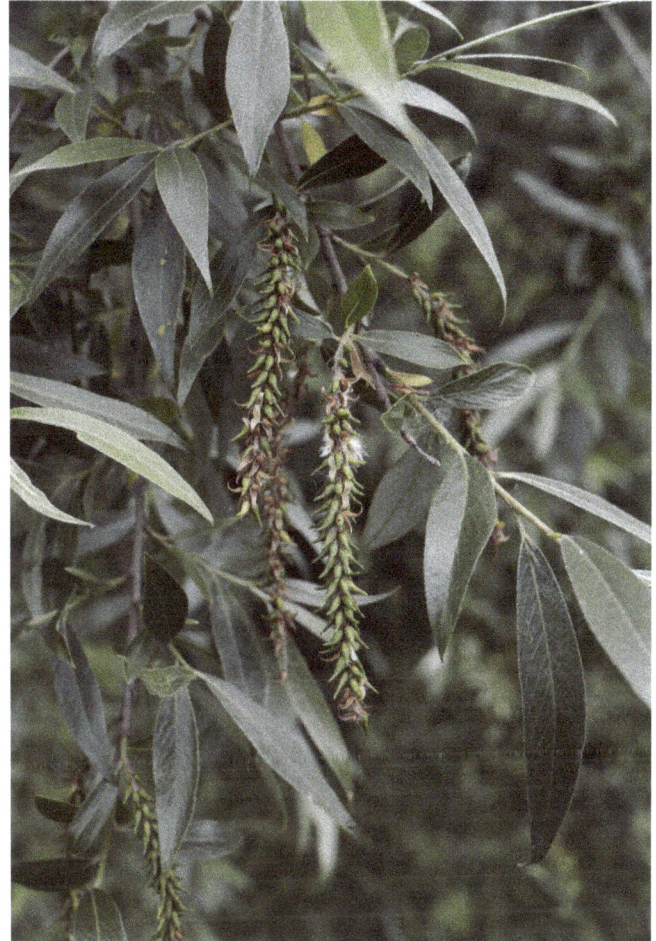

- Eating the tree's bud guarantees health and prosperity throughout the year.
- When casting spells, one must place a circle of willows around themselves as protection from evil entities.
- Putting willow around homes wards off thunder and lightning.
- Sleeping under a willow at night is unwise, because evil forces gather there.
- Wrapping willow around your waist on St. George's Day is done for health and to grow tall and flexible like the willow tree.
- Also on St. George's Day, looking through a crown of willows at the sky will keep storm clouds away.

Other Use: Willows are popular for various Orthodox religious holidays (in the same manner Catholics use palms on Palm Sunday). The willow's bendable wood makes it popular for basket-weaving, and cricket bats are made from the tree's wood. Tannin in the bark made it once used for tanning leather, and charcoal from the wood was an ingredient in making gunpowder. The bark itself is a handy way to tie plants.

A fiber in the stems can be used in paper-making. Cook the fibers with lye for 2 hours, then beat them with mallets or blend them to produce a reddish-brown pulp for paper.

The leaves can be seeped for a tea. The inner bark can be eaten raw or cooked, or dried and ground into a powder that can be added to other flour.

Other Names: European willow, Huntingdon willow, swallow-tailed willow.

Aromatic: Fresh inner bark is bitter, and young leaves or shoots are not palatable. However, they have been eaten as a famine food.

SOURCES

Agapkina, Tatyana Alekseevna. "Деревья в славянской народной традиции: Очерки." [Trees in the Slavic folk tradition: Essays.] Indrik: Moscow, 2019. https://www.academia.edu/45107661/Деревья_в_славянской_народной_традиции_Очерки.

Botanical.com. "Willow, White." https://botanical.com/botanical/mgmh/w/wilwhi22.html.

Green, Garry, compiled by. "Slavic Pagan Wand." http://www.rodnovery.ru/attachments/article/526/slavic-pagan-world.pdf.

MacDermott, Mercia. *Bulgarian Folk Customs*. London and Philadelphia: Jessica Kingsley Publishers, 1998.

Malyuta, A. N. "Священные деревья древних славян." [Sacred trees of the ancient Slavs.] August 16, 2016. https://zvezdakrama.org/svyashhennye-derevya-drevnih-slavyan.

Missouri Botanical Garden. "Salix alba." https://www.missouribotanicalgarden.org/PlantFinder/PlantFinderDetails.aspx?taxonid=286791.

Online Etymology Dictionary. "sallow (n.)." https://www.etymonline.com/search?q=salix.

Petrova, Bilyana, Dr., ed. "Бяла върба." [White willow.] March 18, 2010, updated on April 21, 2022. https://medpedia.framar.bg/ботаника/бяла-върба.

Plants For A Future. "Salix alba - L." https://pfaf.org/user/plant.aspx?latinname=Salix+alba.

Stavreva, Lilia. *Български магии и гадания*. [Bulgarian magic and divination.] Trud Publishing House: Sofia, 2007.

Terzieva, Vasya. "Емил Елмазов разчете древни рецепти от богомилския „Зелейник", които прилага и днес." [Emil Elmazov decoded ancient recipes from the Bogomil 'Zeleinik', which he still uses today.] June 23, 2018. https://www.dnesbg.com/goreshti-novini/emil-elmazov-raztchete-drevni-retsepti-ot-bogomilskiya-vzeleynikv-koito-prilaga-i-dnes.html.

V., Stefan. "The Cult Of The Trees in Slavic Mythology." https://www.slavorum.org/the-cult-of-the-trees-in-slavic-mythology/.

Woodland Trust. "Willow, White." https://www.woodlandtrust.org.uk/trees-woods-and-wildlife/british-trees/a-z-of-british-trees/white-willow/.

ROWAN
Sorbus aucuparia

Sorbus aucuparia
Rowan

⚠️

Rowan has been considered a sacred tree of protection for millennia. Called "The Lady of the Mountain," it's a tree of much symbolism. Its bright-red berries have been equated to blood. It's also a feminine tree, associated with modesty and beauty. Additionally, the tree is said to encourage people to listen to their heart when making a difficult decision, and it signifies a new journey.

Description: Rowan grows to a height of 16 to 49 feet (5 to 15 meters), with a spread of 8 to 23 feet (2.5 to 7 meters). Its crown is narrow, with an upright to oval shape that becomes rounder as it opens with age. The reddish-gray or grayish-green bark is smooth, and the branches are gray. The bark develops lengthwise cracks and flakes as the tree ages.

Green leaves alternate up the twig. They have between nine and fifteen leaflets, which are oblong to lanceolate in shape. Their edges are serrated. They are a darker color on top and are hairy on the underside. In autumn, the leaves turn yellow or reddish-purple to orangish-red in drier areas.

Small white flowers have five elliptical-shaped petals. Blossoms form in dense clusters of around 250 flowers. The buds are hairy, and the flowers produce pea-sized berries that turn from green to scarlet or orange-red as they ripen. Commercial varieties may be pink, yellow, or bright red. The fruits hang in pendant clusters. They contain two to six seeds.

History and Traditions: The genus name is of uncertain origin. It has been suggested it is a derivative of a Proto-Indo-European word for "red." Other thoughts are that it comes from a non-Indo-European word for "berry." The specific name comes from the Latin words *avis* and *capere*, for "bird" and "to catch," respectively, since the fruit was used as bait to capture birds. The common name of rowan is from an old Germanic word *raud-inan* for "to redden."

The tree was sacred to the Druids, as a portal between death and rebirth. In Norse mythology, Thor grabbed a rowan branch to prevent himself from drowning. Plato uses the sorb apple as a metaphor to describe soul mates longing for one another, where human nature was cut in half, one element being male and the other female.

Another soul theme is found in the idea that the rowan was a traveler's tree. Walking sticks made from the hard, dense wood were used by those following a path their soul called them to travel. It helped them find their way home if they became lost. In addition, the person would chew the staff and keep a splinter inside their mouth next to their cheek to protect themselves from sorcery or other dangers in their travels.

Among the Slavs, rowan nights were stormy summer and autumn evenings. In particular, rowan has three special times during the year, called its

CAUTION: Remove the seeds when using the fruit medicinally or as food. The seeds contain cyanogenic glycosides, which produce toxic prussic acid when reacting to water. Large doses of them can cause respiratory failure and death. Also, consuming large amounts of the berries, cooked or raw, can cause upset stomach or vomiting.

birthdays. In spring, around May 25, the tree blooms. This is a time women call on the tree to protect their homes from fire and lightning. If the dawn of this day is red, it predicts summer will be filled with wildfires. The second birthday occurs in summer, not long after the solstice, when the berries appear and begin to ripen. The final one is during autumn, September 23, when the berries have completely ripened and can be harvested for magical and ordinary use. On this day, people hang the tree's branches under roofs and around the edges of fields for protection.

Habitat and Distribution: Native to Europe, northern Africa, and western Asia, and naturalized in Canada and the northern U.S. The tree grows in scrublands or thinned forests in mountainous regions.

Growth: Deciduous tree or shrub. The plant blossoms from May to June, and the fruits ripen around August to September. Lifespans for the trees are around 80 years or even up to 300 to 400 years.

Rowans grow best in moist, well-drained soils that are lighter, and seldom are found in clay or soft limestone. They do best with full sunlight, although they can grow in partial shade. Since they are native to mountainous regions, they are frost tolerant and

---

The Devil's Tree

A folk story tells about how Satan created the red rowan, and that is the reason it has magical properties. God, however, observed that the fruit bore cross-like shapes and that the leaves looked like crosses. He therefore decided the tree was no longer unclean. Ever since then, Satan hated the tree and became afraid of it (Color.mir).

Baba Vanga's Remedies

The late Bulgarian healer and clairvoyant Baba Vanga had many healing recipes to her name. One for anemia is to mix 10 g of nettle leaves (*Urtica dioica*) with 25 g of rowan berries. Then pour 500 ml of boiling water over 1 Tablespoon of the mixture and simmer for 10 minutes. Steep the liquid for 4 hours before straining. Drink a half a cup of the liquid four times a day.

Another recipe for angina pectoris calls for mixing 50 g of rowan berries, 20 g of spearmint (*Mentha spicata*) and 10 g of chamomile (*Matricaria chamomilla*). Then pour 300 ml of boiling water over them and steep for several hours. Strain the liquid and drink the same day (Radev, 11).

do better in cooler climates that lack hot humid summers.

Harvesting: Leaves, bark, flowers, and fruits are used. Harvest them when they're fully ripe. They can be used fresh or dried. Dry in a dehydrator at 95 to 104°F (35 to 40°C) at first, then increase the heat to 131 to 140°F (55 to 60°C). They'll become red-orange, and their surface will be wrinkled and shiny.

Medical Use: Rowan is used in folk medicine. The leaves treat burns, coughs, and stomachaches. They also are used to help reduce kidney stones. The bark is a treatment for diarrhea and to help reduce fatty content in the liver. The berries and flowers are also used to treat diarrhea, and the berries are used for carbon monoxide poisoning, since chewing on them aids the body in increasing oxygen. The berries have a calming effect and help reduce exhaustion. An infusion from the berries (without the seeds) is good to gargle with for a sore throat. Rowan is also used for obesity, hemorrhoids, kidney diseases, diabetes, rheumatism, menstruation, and vitamin C deficiency.

Rituals and Magical Use: The rowan is called the Samodiva or fairy tree (самодивско дърво) among Bulgarians. It was also the tree in which Slavs left notes for the forest spirit called Leshy. In mythology, the tree has a connection with Perun, the supreme Slavic god, since a design on the berries has a resemblance to lightning. As such, a rowan branch is called Perun's club.

It is a tree of harmony, health, and supernatural powers. Rowan protects people against evil beings, bad luck, and witchcraft, since evil spirits shunned the tree. People made magical staffs, amulets, and talismans from the wood. A tree planted near the porch or front gate would protect the home from magical attacks, and the tree would render null any spells cast by witches. Families hung ripe clusters of the berries in front of cattle pens to protect the animals from illness. Mothers also strung rowanberries onto a string or adorned dolls with the berries as a talisman for their children.

When people returned home from a funeral, they hung rowan over their doorway to prevent the deceased from coming back home. A further ritual could be performed if the person was expected to become one of the undead. He was nailed to the ground with a stake made from rowan wood.

Rowan was also used at weddings to protect the newlyweds from jinxes. The plants decorated the location of the ceremony inside and outside. In addition, sprigs adorned the cake, and leaves were hidden in the couple's shoes and pockets. An offering was poured around the roots of a tree to ensure nothing spoiled the wedding. And the bride held rowan roots or a cross as protection from the evil eye.

The tree is also one used for healing. Standing at the roots of the tree and reciting charms was one way to cure a sick person from fever or other diseases. Also, standing under the tree was a way to scare away the illness. Others would cure themselves by climbing over a rowan bush three times. A method of soothing toothaches was to kneel by the tree at sunrise, hug and kiss the tree, and chew on rowan wood while reciting a charm in which the sufferer swore not to eat the tree's berries ever again. To complete the ritual, the person would have to return home without looking back and avoid meeting anyone else on the way. Carrying a piece of rowan wood in one's pocket was believed to cure rheumatism, as well as be a charm against ill wishes.

Even though the tree offered protection and healing, in some places, it was considered unholy or unclean, as it was connected with witches, devils, or werewolves. They would somersault through the tree or over its stump in order to shift into another shape.

The tree was also considered vindictive. If anyone cut or broke its branches, picked the flowers or berries, or used the wood as firewood for no good reason or without the proper ceremony, the person or his family would suffer misfortune. It could be as simple as the person getting a toothache or as serious as contracting a disease or suffering death. Part of this reasoning was because diseases were transferred to the tree. Anyone who did any damage to the tree would therefore take these diseases into himself. Another reason was that a legend says that the first woman on Earth was born from the tree. To cut down the tree meant the cutter or a close relative would soon die.

Rowan is also used as a weather forecaster. A saying is that if the forest is full of red rowan, then autumn will be rainy. In addition, if a tree has lots of berries, winter will be long and frosty.

Other Use: Rowan berries are not as popular as others because they are bitter and hard, but it is used to make jams and preserves, or dried and mixed with cereals to make flour. In Russia, they bake the fresh berries with honey or sugar for an autumn snack. A strong wine was made by scalding the berries with boiling water, then adding yeast to allow the liquid to ferment. Other foodstuffs include

syrup and a drink called *kvass*, as well as using the leaves for tea.

Other uses of the berries are to create an infusion to make dull hair shine. An oil from the seeds is used in cosmetics to make a face mask to fight wrinkles and make the skin look fresh and rosy. The wood is used as a dousing rod and to make mallet handles.

A black dye can be produced from young branches, and all parts of the plant contain tannin. The wood is hard and has fine grains, so it's used for carving and to make barrel hoops, cogs, and furniture.

Other Names: European rowan, European mountain ash, common mountain ash, mountain ash, service tree, rowanberry, quickbeam, whitebeam, sorbus. Synonym: *Pyrus aucuparia*.

Aromatic: The flowers have an unpleasant odor and young leaves smell like marzipan. Dried berries have a slight odor and a bitter or sour taste. Harvesting them after the frost, though, makes them softer and less bitter.

SOURCES

Bilki.bg. "Офика, действие и приложение на билката." [Rowan, action and application of the herb.] https://bilki.bg/encyclopedia-bilki/ofika.html.

Color-mir.com. "Red Rowan in Slavic mythology." https://color-mir.com/red-rowan-in-slavic-mythology/ (link no longer available).

Folkard, Richard, Jr. *Plant Lore, Legends, and Lyrics. Embracing the Myths, Traditions, Superstitions, and Folklore of the Plant Kingdom*. London: S. Low, Marston, Searle, and Rivington, 1884. https://hdl.handle.net/2027/hvd.32044102827375.

Malyuta, A. N. "Священные деревья древних славян." [Sacred trees of the ancient Slavs.] August 16, 2016. https://zvezdakrama.org/svyashhennye-derevya-drevnih-slavyan.

Markov, Al. "Krastova Gora - where faith in God banishes despondency." September 14, 2022. https://bnr.bg/en/post/101704742/krastova-gora-where-faith-in-god-banishes-despondency.

Missouri Botanical Garden. "Sorbus aucuparia." http://www.missouribotanicalgarden.org/PlantFinder/PlantFinderDetails.aspx?taxonid=286370&isprofile=1&basic=sorbus.

Online Etymology Dictionary. "sorb (n.)." https://www.etymonline.com/search?q=Sorbus+aucuparia.

Plants For A Future. "Sorbus aucuparia - L." https://pfaf.org/user/Plant.aspx?LatinName=Sorbus+aucuparia.

Radev, L. *Baba Vanga's Unique Natural Remedies*. https://www.free-ebooks.net/excerpt/Baba-Vanga-s-Unique-Natural-Remedies/html/4.

Stanton, Olga. "Sacred Trees of Slavs: Rowan." September 23, 2021. https://www.facebook.com/slavicmagpie/posts/pfbid02QMKgxHEWHPjLQYxwKSu47AJwppAipR8GX5ryQfJL5mQxvHMy9Vwm9o57hP5rQ27El.

Tree-guide.com. "European Mountain Ash, Rowan." http://www.tree-guide.com/european-mountain-ash-rowan.

Tree Spirit Wisdom. "Rowan – Calling." https://treespiritwisdom.com/tree-spirit-wisdom/rowan-tree-symbolism/.

SILVER LINDEN
Tilia tomentosa

Tilia tomentosa
Silver linden

Called "lipa" among the Bulgarians, this tree is a marvel to behold. It's a favorite of bees, which swarm around the flowers, generating a noticeable humming. The wood, too, creates wonders, and artists love it because they can create minute details on their work.

Description: The linden tree grows to a height of 65 to 130 feet (20 to 40 meters), with a crown spreading 30 to 50 feet (9 to 15 meters). Bark on younger trees is gray and nearly smooth, while the bark on older trees may turn brown and has shallow cracks. The tree has a large crown, and its branches divide and subdivide to create a symmetrical shape.

An abundance of asymmetrical, heart-shaped leaves form, with serrated edges and pointed tips. The upper leaf surface is glossy green, while the underside is silvery-white and covered with hairs. In autumn, the leaves turn yellow.

Pale-yellow flowers have five petals clustered on a slender stalk in groups of two to ten, or up to fifteen in some species. The plant produces round nuts with hard shells and a wing. The tree is known for its rich supply of sap.

History and Traditions: The genus name dates back to the Proto-Indo-European *ptel-eia*, which means "broad" or "broad-leafed," and the specific name means "covered with soft-wooly hairs." The name "linden" comes from the Latin *lentus*, for "flexible."

The tree usually lives a few hundred years, but some have survived for 1,000 (or longer). Throughout the history of many cultures, the tree has been considered sacred. It symbolized love for some. In ancient Greece, two myths tell the story of the linden tree's origin. In one, the nymph Prilyra asked to be turned into the tree when she gave birth to the centaur Chiron after Chronos (as a horse) seduced her. From this form, she taught Chiron wisdom and compassion, and he in turn educated noblemen's sons under the linden tree.

In a second myth, Philemon and Baucis, a married couple, didn't want to be separated at death. Philemon turned into an oak, while Baucis became a linden. The branches of the two trees became intertwined. And so, during the Middle Ages, people would swear their love under the tree's shadow, believing the tree would decide if they told the truth. In addition, small chapels were built under its branches because people believed their prayers would be heard if spoken under the linden, because the tree was favored by the Virgin Mary.

To Germanic tribes, the tree symbolized justice and peace. They held meetings under it, and verdicts in judgments were issued "under Tilia." They also used the wood to make shields.

Habitat and Distribution: Native to the temperate northern hemisphere throughout Europe, Asia, and North America. The trees grow in forests alongside

---

CAUTION: The flowering plant triggers allergies in some people. Using flowers that are too old in tisanes may produce symptoms of narcotic intoxication.

beech and oak and by themselves along roads or in open spaces.

Growth: Deciduous tree. It flowers in early June or July, and the nuts ripen in summer. The tree can grow in different climates and soil types, but it prefers moist, fertile soils that are well-drained. It grows best in full sun, but it can tolerate partial shade. Linden is drought tolerant and can exist in urban conditions.

Harvesting: Flowers, leaves, and bark are used. Pick the flowers on a sunny, dry day before noon. When most of the flowers have dissolved, but some have not yet blossomed, gather the ones that are currently blooming. Be careful not to crush the flowers while picking them, so they don't darken while they dry. Dry them in the shade or in a dehydrator at 113°F (45°C). They are ready when their handles become brittle. Store them in a cool, dark place in a closed container or in a cloth or plastic bag.

Medical Use: Linden is described as a tree with healing powers concentrated in its flowers. Mostly, the flowers are made into an infusion or distilled water for household remedies. Common treatments

---

Origin of the Bear

In a northern Russian tale, a man was going to cut down a linden tree. The tree, however, begged him to refrain. In return, she would give him whatever he desired. The man told his wife about the talking tree. The woman was conceited and demanded that the tree give them wealth. This was granted. Later, the wife told him to ask the tree to make everyone afraid of the two of them. The tree did, but not in the way the couple expected. The linden turned them into bears (Agapkina, 120).

Linden Honey

Honey made from linden is light yellow. Taken internally, it's good for the digestive system and has anti-inflammatory benefits. People also take it for visual problems and bladder and kidney inflammation. Externally, it can be applied to injuries, eczema, and burns.

Be careful to take only small doses and not too often, especially if you suffer from diabetes or allergies. It contains a lot of female hormones, so men should limit their consumption (Petrova).

Old trees have been called saints. These are one of the species that people were forbidden from cutting down. To do so, meant death—either to the cutter or to someone in his family. A man who broke a branch from a tree was said to have gone berserk. He recovered only after he returned the branch. Others who cut down the tree became lost in the forest.

Stories circulated about trees that bled blood and not sap. One such tree was born out of a knee of a girl who was killed. This tree stood on the top of a mountain. Local people venerated it, much to the dismay of a priest. When he tried to cut it down, blood coming out of the tree blinded him.

Linden is a sacred tree of lovers and fertility, and marriages are still conducted under the tree. And linden is used in divination and spells about love. Planting a tree in front of your house protects the family from evil spirits and lightning, and it also helps people not be overwhelmed by temptations. Its wood is used against vampires. Native Siberians planted a linden tree near their home as a means to reach the realms of the underworld and the heavens.

The tree could also be used for harmful magic. A witch could turn someone into a werewolf by pouring a decoction of linden bark over him. In addition, on Kupula, those who wanted to turn themselves into wolves would tear bark from the tree and whip themselves with the branches.

A popular saying was, "The linden dried up in the garden, for worse." It was considered a tragedy to lose a linden, not only because of its healing capacity but also because the tree served other purposes. It provided honey, and bast (inner bark) shoes were woven from it. In addition, handicrafts were made from various parts of the tree. It was an essential part of rural life and survival.

Among various cultures, the tree symbolizes not only love and fertility but also prosperity, fidelity,

are for respiratory problems like laryngitis, bronchitis, and coughs. Baths made with the infused flowers are recommended for hysteria, and linden tea with honey is good before sleeping, because it has a calming, soothing effect on body and mind. Linden is also a treatment for urinary problems, hemorrhoids, skin diseases, dizziness, headaches, anemia, high blood pressure, muscle spasms, and hair loss.

Rituals and Magical Use: Linden is one of the most magical trees, especially among Slavs. The tree is dedicated to Svetovid, the Slavic god of war and abundance.

friendship, justice, altruism, and good luck. It's believed that linden flowers and branches placed around the home will ward off evil spirits and bring peace. In the bedroom, it promotes fertility, fidelity, and a long marriage. The tree symbolizes a divine presence. Sick people stand under the tree, hoping to be healed. Linden is also used to make "living fire," used for purification rituals.

Other Use: Linden honey is included in medicines and liqueurs, while the flower's essential oil is an ingredient in perfumes, cosmetics (creams, soaps, shampoos), aromatherapy, floral decorations, and dye. Young leaves and leaf buds are edible raw. The inner bark is used for matting, baskets, and fishing nets. Linden is a soft wood, has little grain, is relatively lightweight, and is made into furniture, intricate wood carvings, models, puppets, bodies of electric and bass guitars, wind instruments, drum shells, and window shutters.

Other Names: European white lime, silver lime, white lime (not related to the lime fruit).

Aromatic: The flowers are fragrant, fresh and dried, and the fruit is sweet and sticky.

SOURCES

Agapkina, Tatyana Alekseevna. "Деревья в славянской народной традиции: Очерки." [Trees in the Slavic folk tradition: Essays.] Indrik: Moscow, 2019. https://www.academia.edu/45107661/Деревья_в_ славянской_народной_традиции_Очерки.

Botanical.com. "Lime Tree." https://botanical.com/botanical/mgmh/l/limtre28.html.

Green, Garry. "Slavic Pagan World." http://www.rodnovery.ru/attachments/article/526/slavic-pagan-world. pdf.

Just Fun Facts. "Interesting facts about linden trees." 2017. http://justfunfacts.com/interesting-facts-about-linden-trees/.

Malyuta, A. N. "Священные деревья древних славян." [Sacred trees of the ancient Slavs.] August 16, 2016. https://zvezdakrama.org/svyashhennye-derevya-drevnih-slavyan.

Missouri Botanical Garden. "Tilia tomentosa." http://www.missouribotanicalgarden.org/PlantFinder/ PlantFinderDetails.aspx?taxonid=287372&isprofile=1&basic=Tilia%20tomentosa.

Path to the Maypole of Wisdom. "Symbolism of the linden tree." https://maypoleofwisdom.com/the-symbolism-of-the-linden-tree/.

Petrova, Bilyana, Dr., ed. "Липа." [Linden.] April 7, 2010, updated on August 19, 2021. https://medpedia. framar.bg/ботаника/липа.

V., Stefan. "The Cult Of The Trees in Slavic Mythology." https://www.slavorum.org/the-cult-of-the-trees-in-slavic-mythology/.

Willow. "Herbarium: Magical and Medicinal Use of Linden." April 5, 2021. https://www.flyingthehedge.com/ 2021/04/magical-and-medicinal-use-of-linden.html.

ELM

Ulmus minor

Ulmus minor
Elm

History and Traditions: The genus name is the Latin word for elm, which has a connection with the Sanskrit root for "to grow." The specific name is Latin for "less" or "lesser."

Elm trees are associated with death, and an old British saying is, "Elm hateth man and waiteth." This has two common meanings. One has to do with the possibility that branches that suddenly fell from large trees hit people. The second is that elm was used to make coffins, since the wood was durable underground.

The tree was sacred to Druid priests, and to the Knights Templar. It was believed to grant people prophetic powers. In Germanic mythology, it was called "Embla" and represented the name of the first woman. Elm was a tree of dreams in Greek mythology and was associated with Morpheus, the god of dreams. French called the elm the tree of justice, and preachers and judges would be inspired beneath its branches.

Since the wood can withstand wet conditions, elm was popular in boat-building, bridge foundations, and cart wheels. The wood was also used to make longbows. Additionally, before wide use of metals, hollowed-out elm was used for water mains.

Medically, liquid from boiled inner bark was a treatment for colds and sore throats, and the boiled bark itself was used on burns.

Habitat and Distribution: Native to central and southern Europe, northern Africa, and south-western Asia. It has also been naturalized in North America. The tree grows in woods, plains, slopes, and uncultivated land, as well as along riverbeds.

Growth: Deciduous tree. Elm blossoms around February or March, and fruits mature in summer.

Elm is a tree that tends to bounce back even after diseases wipe out many of its species. From the Dutch Elm Disease of the 1960s to a plague that wiped out elms in the Roman Empire, elms have continued to survive through sucker roots that sprout up even after the main tree has died.

Description: This elm has a height of around 65 to 130 feet (20 to 40 meters), with a broad, fan-shaped to oval crown, spreading to an average of 62 feet (19 meters). The tree's branches are long and intertwined. A young tree has smooth bark that turns dark-gray or brownish-gray and cracked as it ages.

Asymmetrical glossy bright-green leaves form on short stalks. The leaves are ovate, double-serrated, and pointed at the tip. They contain eight to thirteen pronounced lateral veins. In autumn, the leaves turn yellow.

Dark-pink to purplish-red flowers appear before the leaves. They grow in dense groups of fifteen to thirty that hang in tassels. They form small, dry winged fruits called samaras, which are initially green but turn brown as they mature.

CAUTION: No known hazards, but always consult with a medical professional before using herbs medicinally. Pregnant and lactating women should avoid use due to lack of information on its safety.

Elm prefers full sun and moist, deep clay soil, with good drainage, but it can grow in poor soils. The tree tolerates floods, droughts, frost, strong winds, and air pollution. Although it is prone to disease, it sends out many sucker roots, and is fast growing.

Harvesting: Bark is used. Collect inner bark from branches of trees that are three to four years old.

Dry them for later use and store them in a dry location.

Medical Use: Elm bark has anti-inflammatory and astringent properties. It's a treatment for digestive disorders, severe diarrhea, rheumatism, hemorrhoids, and also to reduce water retention. An external application is for cleaning infected

---

An Orpheus and Eurydice HEA Tale

It's perhaps the elm's ability to survive through hardships that connects it to the story of Orpheus and Eurydice. The tale you may know is one where Orpheus goes to Hades to retrieve his wife, who had died from a snake bite. With his music, he convinces the god of the dead to let Eurydice leave. The condition is that he must not look back until they both are in the land of the living again. At the last moment, Orpheus looks back, and his wife must return to the land of the dead. In that spot, the first elm sprang up.

But, there's another side to this story, a Thracian one, which has a happier ending. While standing over Eurydice's grave, Orpheus looked up to the sky, then reached his staff down to touch his beloved's hand, commanding her, "Hold on to my wand and return to the world of the living."

And she did. Thus revived, she responded, "Thank you, Orpheus, for coming to me only in the realm of the dead to bring me back to life. Yes, you came to the dark wall and the moat that separates the worlds—where are the stars that do not rise or set and there is no sunlight. You called me by name in the impenetrable darkness and held out your hand to me in the abyss. You walk the steep path for me, risking your own life. Your love saved me and my heart belongs only to you, because I loved you, too."

He brought her out of the grave and hid her from his enemies, who proclaimed to the world that he had failed. But, like the elms that die and revive, so did Eurydice, for she was a dryad after all (Tomašova-Ivanova, Trees for Life).

wounds. You can use a decoction to rinse your mouth to treat sores or even wash your scalp to treat baldness.

Elm is another one of Bach's Thirty-eight Flowers. Its purpose is to help those who feel inadequate or are exhausted from trying to be perfect.

Rituals and Magical Use: Elms have a wide range of symbolism: victory, achievement, vision, divination, prophecy, aspirations, intuition, romantic love, friendship, strength, longevity, and more. Brides ask the tree for fruitfulness, while the leaves are made into children's beds to strengthen their bones and joints. This magical tree brings order, courage, and solutions and protects against evil.

Elms also have an association with the underworld: Orpheus in Greek mythology and elves who guarded burial mounds and their dead in Celtic.

Among the Bulgarians, while willows are a favorite place for Rusalki (water maidens) to play, woodland nymphs, called Samodivi or Samovili, prefer to picnic and dance under elms.

The ritual fortune-telling called "live coals" that you learned about in oaks was also possible using elms. Additionally, sick people would crawl around on the roots of an elm to "remove" their illness. And a person with chronic fatigue could ask a witch to transfer the ailment to the tree.

Other Use: Elm's wood is hard and durable, lacks knots, and resists abrasions, so it's often used to make furniture, doors, and flooring, as well as used in boats. The tough fiber from the inner bark is suitable for making mats and ropes. The trees can be trained into bonsais.

The plant's leaves are edible, either raw or cooked, and are used for tea. Elm's fruit can be eaten raw as soon as it is formed. Inner bark can be boiled, then dried and ground into a powder to thicken soups or added to cereal flour.

Other Names: Field elm, smooth-leaved elm, European field elm. Synonyms: *Ulmus carpinifolia* and *Ulmus campestris*.

Aromatic: Leaves are bitter, especially the older ones, and they have a slimy texture. Immature fruits are fragrant. They make the mouth feel fresh and breath smell nice.

SOURCES

Caro, Tina. "Elm Tree Symbolism and Meaning [With Birth Date Symbolism]." https://magickalspot.com/elm-tree-symbolism-meaning/.

Ecosostenibile. "Ulmus minor." December 15, 2022. https://antropocene.it/en/2022/12/15/ulmus-minor-2/.

Framar.bg. "Бряст полски." [Field elm.] April 8, 2010, updated on January 7, 2021. https://medpedia.framar.bg/ботаника/бряст-полски.

MacDermott, Mercia. *Bulgarian Folk Customs*. London and Philadelphia: Jessica Kingsley Publishers, 1998.

Nottinghamscience. "Elm – The Tree of Death." https://www.youtube.com/watch?v=OEtadNu61ZQ.

Ristic, Radomir. *Balkan Traditional Witchcraft*. Los Angeles: Pendraig Publishing, 2009.

Tomašova-Ivanova, Nina. "Митът за „Орфей и Евридика"– скритата история." [The myth of "Orpheus and Eurydice" – the hidden story." July 27, 2029. https://eklekti.com/mityt-za-orfei-i-evridika-skritata-istoriya/.

Trees for Life. "Elm mythology and folklore." https://treesforlife.org.uk/into-the-forest/trees-plants-animals/trees/elm/elm-mythology-and-folklore/.

Van der Berk Nurseries. "Ulmus minor." https://www.vdberk.com/trees/ulmus-minor/.

Woodland Trust. "Elm, Field." https://www.woodlandtrust.org.uk/trees-woods-and-wildlife/british-trees/a-z-of-british-trees/field-elm/.

Harvesting Herbs

If you want herbs to work effectively, then you must harvest them at certain times and under the best possible conditions. I'm not talking about under a full moon while chanting. I'm sure there are many ways to gather herbs for magical purposes, and perhaps that will be a future book. What I'm talking about is gathering herbs to use medically.

The medical substances are distributed differently throughout a plant's parts. Sometimes, the leaves have the highest concentration; other times, it's the roots, flowers, or fruit, or bark on trees and shrubs. Not only that, but other conditions affect the plant's strength: weather, soil type, plant age.

The trees in this book have already provided some examples, but it is not meant to be a guide on harvesting herbs. If you're serious about attempting this, make sure to research the herb thoroughly. Consult with an experienced herbalist. Talk to a holistic practitioner. Make sure you do your due diligence. Don't attempt to gather herbs that have ANY poisonous substances on your own. Let a trained herbalist do that.

Mistakes can be fatal!

Some general rules follow about best practices for harvesting herbs. They come from Ivanov's *Herbs in Bulgaria and Their Use*, pages 29 to 34.

When to Gather

It's best to collect the herbs when the weather is dry and sunny, after the dew has evaporated, in order to prevent them from becoming moldy.

- **Roots**: Autumn, after the aboveground part has withered or early spring before it starts to grow.
- **Buds**: Early spring before they open.
- **Flowers**: Either right before they open fully or when they've completely blossomed.
- **Fruits**: Fully ripe and whole. Avoid them if they're rotten, damaged, or insect-eaten.
- **Bark**: Autumn, after the fruit ripens or early spring before the tree's juices flow.

Process for Gathering

For both your safety and the plant's, here are suggestions for the best practices when collecting herbs.

- Don't touch your eyes, nose, mouth, and ears while you are picking herbs.
- Wash your hands thoroughly when you have finished.
- Many species are endangered or protected, so don't pick them.
- Don't over-pick herbs. Only gather as many as you will use during a year's time. They lose their strength if kept longer.
- Be careful not to pull up plants that propagate by roots, unless you are harvesting roots. Even then, take only small amounts so the plant can regenerate.
- Pick only one type of herb at a time, so you don't mix them.
- Use a basket to avoid crushing the herbs.

Drying Herbs

You have various options for drying herbs. You can use a dehydrator, or dry them naturally in the shade or inside. If you use a room in your house, it must be well-ventilated and dry. Start the drying process within five or six hours after gathering the herbs. You don't want to dry them in the sun, because it destroys the plant's chlorophyll.

- **Above-ground parts**: Dry until they start to break, not bend.
- **Roots**: Cut and chop thick, fleshy roots, then dry until they start to break when folded.

The temperature you dry the plants at varies by the type of plant you are drying.

- **Contain essential oils**: Dry at 86° to 104°F (30° to 40°C).
- **Fleshy fruits**: Dry at 140° to 212°F (60° to 100°C).
- **Everything else**: Dry at 113° to 167°F (45° to 75°C).

Storing Herbs

It's best to store them in airtight containers, in a dark, dry place. As with picking the herbs, you want to avoid them getting moldy.

SOURCE

Ivanov, Ivan Isaev, Prof.; Iliya Ivanov Landzhev, Dr. of Pharmacy; Geo Kirilov Neshev, Dr. of Medicine. *Билките в България и използването им.* [Herbs in Bulgaria and their use.] Zemizdat: Sofia, 1977.

About the Author

Ronesa Aveela is "the creative power of two." Two authors, that is. Nelly, the main force behind the work, the creative genius, was born in Bulgaria and moved to the U.S. in the 1990s. She grew up with stories of wild Samodivi, Kikimora, the dragons Zmey and Lamia, Baba Yaga, and much more. She's a freelance artist and writer. She likes writing mystery romance inspired by legends and tales. In her free time, she paints. Her artistic interests include the female figure, Greek and Thracian mythology, folklore tales, and the natural world interpreted through her eyes. She is married and has two children.

Rebecca, her writing partner, was born and raised in the New England area. She has a background in writing and editing, as well as having a love of all things from different cultures. She's learned so much about Bulgarian culture, folklore, and rituals, and writes to share that knowledge with others.

Connect with us at www.ronesaaveela.com!

Would you like to learn more about folklore and mythology? Visit our website and sign up for our periodic newsletter to get updates about book releases and promotions.

www.ingramcontent.com/pod-product-compliance
Lightning Source LLC
Chambersburg PA
CBHW042338030426

42335CB00030B/3393